Serviced Accommodation Secrets

Starting and Scaling Your Rent to Rent SA
Business to £10K a Month & Beyond

Hugo Bennings

Table of Contents

Free Deal Analyser
Spreadsheet

Use this spreadsheet to analyse ALL of the R2R deals that you're about to learn how to source, negotiate and secure in this book.

(It's the exact same spreadsheet that I've used to 'stack' hundreds of deals and make a lot of money in the process!)

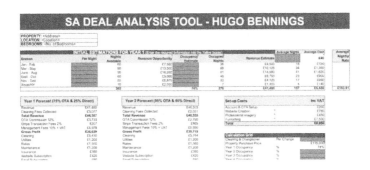

Go to https://bit.ly/2XNHoaU and grab your free Excel spreadsheet now. No email address required. It's going to make it really easy for you to know which deals are worth pursuing – and which you should ignore. It's my way of saying thank you, to you, for purchasing this book and trusting in me to show you the ways of the R2R road.

Without any further ado, let's get to the **Serviced Accommodation Secrets.**

Introduction

There are so many brits who complain and whine about how difficult it is to start investing in the UK property market. And they're not entirely wrong. At one point, I was convinced it was impossible too. With so much information online about the many advantages of investing, all the success stories of property millionaires and billionaires; who wouldn't want to jump in and get a piece of the pie? Residential portfolios, commercial property, office space, cash-flowing apartment blocks, real estate investment trusts (property stocks) - there's a tremendous amount of options. The only challenge that inhibits people from jumping in, building wealth and earning passive income - is the massive amount of capital that's typically needed to invest. The average residential house in the UK costs £233,000, and many people cannot even afford a 10% deposit on a home this expensive - as demonstrated through the one million+ people on the council waiting list for social housing, and the millions more living in private rented accommodation. The biggest hurdle in property investing is raising the hefty deposit required. Investment properties normally require 25% down, making it even harder to save enough of a deposit. Scale this up to apartment blocks or prime city-centre office buildings, and there's only a select few who can invest in such assets. So, where does that leave you and me?

In my early life, I went through significant financial hardship which taught me a hell of a lot. I grew up pretty fast – more on that later. These tough times also made me realise that I'd remain poor forever if I only relied on my salary from my full-time IT job. I wanted to become wealthy, like many, so that I could stop living month to month and so that I could provide my family with everything that they needed, and that I never had. But from my salary alone I was not in a position to save much, if anything at all - to enable me to make any meaningful investments. If you are like me, and you have faced financial difficulties that have awoken you to the need of making investments that provide monthly passive income, then you will understand the incredible value and opportunity that property investing presents. The amount of money that is typically needed, however, leads many to give up on their dreams of owning and managing property in the United Kingdom.

Despite the financial hurdle, do you still have hopes of discovering an investment strategy where you can earn monthly cash flow, in addition to your salary? Or maybe even make so much more money from a side-business, so that you can afford to quit your 9-5 job? Despite your limitations on capital, do you want a property business that you can outsource and one that is flexible to such an extent that you can work from anywhere in the world? Do you want to take action and start making investments that will earn significant sums of money, enabling you to even then go out and *buy* your own investment properties in the near future? If you've answered yes to any or all of these questions, then you've come to the right place. The Rent to Rent

HUGO BENNINGS

business model could well be the solution that changes your life, like it has mine. If you don't know already; In summary, the R2R model entails that you find a landlord who is willing to rent you his/her property, which you will then let to one or more tenants. The idea behind the business is to earn more rental income from your tenants or nightly guests than what the landlord is charging you. Through this model, you can make anywhere from £500 to £1,500+ per 'unit' in profit each month - depending on occupancy.

Why is R2R so attractive? For starters, there are no capital barriers to entry, so you don't need large sums of capital saved up to get started. You do not need to apply for a mortgage, so your credit score, how much money you are currently earning, the length of time you have been employed, or whether you are a permanent employee or contract worker doesn't determine your eligibility to make money here. All you need to bring to the table is motivation, a thirst for success, and a good mentor who will help you learn the ropes. This is where I'm (via this book) here to help you. And before you cry out 'But Sub-Letting is ILLEGAL!' – it's not, when you have the right contracts and agreements in place. It's perfectly acceptable, both legally and morally! Like ANY business, it's a case of adding value and being paid in proportion to the quality of the service or product that you provide.

I walked this path (pretty much) alone and learnt some harsh lessons the hard way. But, I am thankful to say that I finally made it. Every month, my Rent to Rent business generates more than £10,000 in profit. In hindsight, I realise that my journey wouldn't have taken so long if I knew what I now know before I started my business. Through my experience, I can tell you how well this strategy works, and this is ultimately what motivated me to write this book. In this book, you will learn everything that; if implemented diligently will take you from a beginner and complete novice in the Rent to Rent Business, to being able to secure your first few deals on your own. The book has all the techniques that you need to start in this business and is laid out in a step-by-step chronological order so that you can avoid the mistakes that many newcomers make at the start. I've no online courses to sell you, no '£X,997 Mentorship Programmes', and none of the other classic marketing rip-offs to shove at you. I simply want to pass on my experience, to share the power of this highly cash-flowing, alternative investment strategy.

Through this strategy, and what you'll read here, you can blow up your business to the point where you are making six- figures a year, profit – and beyond. It won't be easy, but my gosh it will be worth it.

Being able to generate a minimum of £750+ per month from each and every unit you have under management is nothing short of life-changing. Keep reading and you'll learn about the mindset that you need to succeed in this business, how to conduct research prior to commencing your business, choosing clients, setting up, listing the apartment, the operational side of things, packaging deals to others for chunks of cash, and so much more. There is a whole world of opportunity in the short-stay industry, and I want you to get your slice of the pie. The only pre-requisite for success is having the knowledge, followed by diligent implementation. All of the knowledge for you to go out and win is contained inside this book, with no upsells to expensive training courses. It just comes down to following the advice given in this book and applying *exactly* what you learn! Most don't do the 'apply' part, but I'm betting on you to be the rare breed who does.

Just from reading this book, you will with time, be able to create an incredibly passive and high-cash flowing business that can change your life with enough hard work, persistence, and creativity. Ensure that you finish reading the book because you don't want to miss out on the 'secrets of the game', which you can find in Chapter 10. It's packed with tips that you won't find anywhere else, and these are going to be massively valuable to you when you apply them to your Rent to Rent Serviced Accommodation business.

Chapter 1:
How I Got Into This
Strategy & The Mindset
You Need

A Little Backstory

I knew, like many, that property could be the answer to many of my financial problems. I knew that countless people who'd come before me had built generational wealth as well as substantial passive income through property investing. Each blog, book and article I was reading was only reinforcing what I already knew – that financial freedom was attainable and realistic – even for the average joe like me. But there was still something missing. I knew the 'what'. What I was missing was the 'how' part. How do I start making passive income? How do I pull this off in just a few spare hours I had each day? How do I do it without any experience, or well-placed and highly-connected friends? I had *that* inkling that property could be the answer, that inkling which so many of us share. But the few articles or blogs that did mention sources of passive income in property only made reference to rental income from owned-properties, trusts, commercial property, or dividends from REITs, etc. Again, all of these required significant upfront capital investments which I simply didn't have when I was getting started.

While pondering these questions, I was stuck in a tedious, laborious, 9-5, IT job that was highly demanding but which also didn't pay me what I felt that I was worth. I was also working as a part-time freelance writer. What? Yes, I was motivated. Being a father of two, with the third on the way, I knew that life was about to change drastically (and not in a positive way!) for my family unless I did something to change our circumstances. I was approaching 40 years old, and life was… okay. Not great, but okay. Me and my wife had found a rhythm that worked for us and for our two babies. This rhythm was the result of many compromises that we were forced to make, to ensure that we were giving our two babies the best we could, given our financial circumstances. Well, the kids themselves were oblivious that we were living from paycheck to paycheck and that for us, to afford the few paid-for extracurricular activities that we allowed them to do, we had to do without certain things. We'd given up our weekly dinner dates. I had also stopped going out for drinks with my pals and had also sold my old Audi to get a smaller, cheaper to run car. And then, just as we were thinking that we were getting by - we found out that we were having a third!

When I heard the news, I felt all of the walls closing in on me. I tried to smile through it, but I could barely breathe. I started to sweat profusely, and I was extremely anxious. Although an incredible blessing, I was highly concerned that this would be a burden on our already-tight finances. Fortunately, with time, this feeling of utter dread began to push me out of my comfort zone. The more I thought about it, the more I realised that all along, I had assumed that we were part of the middle class when, in fact, we were poor. This was a bitter pill to swallow. But I had to swallow it. It was at this low point in my life, where I finally realised that the only person who was responsible for my family's financial circumstances - was me! I had to take charge. That day, I immediately started researching how to change our financial situation, and this was when I discovered this ultimate yet seemingly elusive goal - financial freedom. From my research, I came up with a straightforward blueprint that I was eager to implement.

1. Look for some means to increase my earning capacity.

2. Avoid procrastination - start now to work and increase income.

3. Cut out all unnecessary expenditure to create room for savings.

4. Save, save, and save some more.

5. With these savings, aim to clear all debt, starting with high interest and non-productive debt, e.g. credit card debt.

6. Work on improving credit score.

7. When debt-free, use a low-capital-input business model to accumulate cash, and cash flow to free up some time.

8. Continue saving until I had enough money to start making investments that can yield true passive income.

9. Don't tire, and don't stop until financial freedom is attained.

I was excited. I was no longer going to act like the victim in the story of my life. This was me, finally about to do something to change the trajectory of my life. At first, everything seemed doable. But, you see, between my job, the freelance writing I was doing and executing on my new plan - I was no longer available for my family. I was stressed, and my wife was tense because it now seemed I was not available for her at a time when she needed me by her side. I was earning some money on the side, but the problem was that our expenses seemed to have ballooned more than what I was making! Between the doctor's visits and the baby preparation, I was whipping out my credit card more often than I wanted to. With each day I felt more and more hopeless. At this rate, I started thinking, was I ever going to achieve financial independence? Granted, I had started working towards this dream now, but how much harder did I have to work to make it? Was I too old? Too uneducated? Maybe I was. I couldn't imagine keeping up this hectic lifestyle where I was chasing more additional income to the point where I no longer had time for my family. I was already tired. And I was scared that maybe, I was burning out.

I regretted this train of thought - as consequences of burning out flashed before my eyes. I wasn't taking good care of myself by working this hard. What if I had a heart attack or a stroke? All the sources of income I had created demanded that I physically show up at work, or that I be tied down to a desk somewhere, typing away. If for some reason, I could not work anymore, what would happen? Who would take care of me and my family? I was losing it. No matter how hard I tried to stifle these feelings, they kept bubbling back up. This was not something that I could ignore. It was during one of these self-introspection sessions when I made up my mind that this was not the ideal way to live. I had a firm belief that there must be something out there that could earn passive income for me and my family, without me working myself to the bone. I KNEW deep down that there was a better way. *I just had to find it!* I went back to doing research online - and read through blog after blog until I stumbled upon the Rent to Rent model. I remember thinking, "This is it. I think I have struck gold." The rest, as they say, is history.

At that time, I also came across a newspaper article which dubbed this Rent to Rent model as "the latest property get-rich-quick-scheme". When I started, I wanted to get rich, and quick. But, having been through the hassle of trying to increase my income for the past few months, let me be upfront with you. Let me tell you that this is the wrong way of looking at this business model. Riches won't just fall in your lap without you working hard. The difference with this R2R strategy was, I could tell that if I worked hard up front, I could create multiple passive income streams, allowing me to spend a little time with my family. That's all I wanted to do. I was prepared to roll up my sleeves and get to work. But my main challenge was that there was very little freely available information about how to succeed in this business model, and so I learnt the hard way. In this book I've documented the lessons, the successes, the secrets, the failures, and the blow-outs – so that your journey to passive income, financial freedom and an incredible life doesn't have to be as painful and as topsy-turvy as my journey was.

Mindset

Not everybody who tries the Rent to Rent business model succeeds. Ultimately, the difference between those who make it (in any business) and those who don't, lies in their mindset. Understanding what it takes to succeed will help you go into the business well-equipped mentally to deal with challenges that you'll inevitably face. In the following section, I'll address some of the most common misconceptions that people have about the Rent to Rent model - so that you start this business with a winning mindset.

You Can Succeed Overnight. Wrong.

If you are in the market for get-rich-quick property deals, which are more analogous to arbitrage or flipping - i.e. 'buy low, sell high, and collect your profits immediately,' then Rent to Rent is probably not for you. You MUST start this business knowing that you will need to commit a lot of research and gain some key skills before you sign your first deal with a landlord to sub-let his or her property. You will then need to put in a lot of hard work to ensure that the property will be well-managed and taken care of. You'll need to form a team of people around you, whom you'll need to constantly manage so that the property yields the maximum possible revenue – allowing you to relax later and spend time with your family or doing whatever you so choose. None of this happens overnight. You'll also need to be on standby to make tough decisions – an example of one of these decisions is choosing to pull the plug on a deal if the anticipated cash flow isn't being realised. You can work this break clause into the deal contract, but I'll show you how to do that later on in the book.

As I say, success with the Rent to Rent model doesn't, and won't come overnight. Continued work is needed to keep the business running at its highest potential. Are there new ways to market your business online to ensure that you are visible and are showing off all of your competitive advantages? (many of which you'll learn in this book?) Is your pricing strategy still right for that area, at that time of year? Are there other property deals in your pipeline to ensure that if a landlord abandons his/her side of the lease agreement, you will remain in business, and still have properties that cashflow positively? There are a lot more considerations that you need to be aware of, that will be discussed in the following chapters. But the key takeaway point here is that you shouldn't walk into this business thinking that you will be able to attain financial freedom and a dream lifestyle without hard work and continued commitment to success.

Once You Have Bookings Coming In, Your Work Is Done. Wrong.

Flows of cash will ONLY keep coming in if you put in the effort to maintain them. As you go into Rent to Rent, keep in mind that you're not the first, and won't be the last fortunate individual to discover this unique business model. There is much competition out there. Not only competition from other people in the Rent to Rent business like you, but also those who offer accommodation to the same target market that you have set your eyes on. Think hotels, guest houses, glamping etc, etc. When you have revenue and bookings coming in, instead of kicking up your feet and relaxing - you need to roll up your sleeves to defend and expand that cash flow. Failure to do so will result in increased vacancy rates and in you having to reduce your nightly prices to boost occupancy – affecting your profit margin. So, it's incredibly important for you to approach the Rent to Rent model as a business that requires you to keep up to date with market trends and also to move with the tide, to continue hitting your monthly profit targets.

Once You Have One Successful Rent to Rent Deal, You Are Set For Life. Wrong.

You can't possibly achieve all of the long-term financial goals with just one good R2R deal. Your first successful deal will instead serve to fundamentally highlight that this business model works and that it's scalable. Each deal that you secure is capped by a contract that lasts for between 3-5 years. You have no guarantee that the owner of the house (the Landlord) will renew the lease past the initial contract. Even if the deal gets renewed, the terms may be different, and not necessarily in your favour. As such, ensure that you don't go into the Rent to Rent business assuming it to be the solution to all of your problems - else you will be disappointed. Instead, walk into it with your eyes wide open and use the first deal as a stepping stone to the next, then the next, then the next, and then to future business opportunities that will come your way. Each of these deals will lead you closer towards achieving your financial independence dream.

As we now know all too well from the recent global pandemic, we also have minimal control over economic fundamentals, and thus we can't predict what may affect a deal a year or two, or three from now. So, don't put all your eggs in one basket, or one deal, and then sit back thinking you've made it! The mojitos on the beach in the tropics will come but not after just ONE deal.

What Do You Need to Bring to the Table?

Are you highly motivated? R2R requires a hungry, motivated individual, with a zeal for success. I came from a situation where failure was not an option, and this was what pushed me to go out there and make something of myself. I had family pressures that were keeping me on my toes, forcing me to make it work. I got the first deal and that initial success boosted my confidence and propelled me to the next deal.

Even when I didn't get the desired outcome, I had it in me to learn from my mistakes and try again. If you are well-motivated and aren't the kind of person to just hang up your boots and sulk in a corner when things aren't going your way, then you have the right mindset. Whatever your motivation is, and whether it's coming from a place of hurt, or a place of abundance - embrace it and convince yourself that you CAN do this.

Are you a hard worker? Are you adaptable to change? Can you think outside the box? Are you a good person? Do you have a small amount of cash set aside to kickstart your Rent to Rent venture? If you proclaimed 'YES!' to at least some of these questions, then the good news is that you have what it takes to make it! Throughout this book, there's a whole host of real-life examples that will show you that you do in fact, have what it takes to make the leap into the Rent to Rent world. So, if you are motivated, prepared to work hard and are willing to learn how to acquire the skills that you don't yet have, buckle up… you're in for an incredible ride! Let's begin!

Chapter 2:
Basics of Serviced
Accommodation

As you start your serviced accommodation business, don't make the mistake of thinking that success is guaranteed. This is a business and all businesses have associated risks, stresses, and at least a small amount of financial investment. You will need to work hard to recover both the money and time that you are investing into your business, even if the money in question is to pay for insurance, pay to be legally compliant, and pay for your phone bill. Things will inevitably go wrong, so be mentally prepared for a ride of ups and downs. To guard against these downs, do your research first and be thorough. Hopefully with the knowledge you'll learn in this book, you will experience far more of the wonderful ups!

Types of Serviced Accommodation

Serviced accommodation, by definition, refers to providing a service of fully-furnished, short-stay living space with amenities like a cleaning service, a fully equipped kitchen, a TV with entertainment subscriptions, Wi-Fi, and all utilities, e.g. water and electricity. This accommodation can be available for anywhere between one night, to three months or more. A serviced apartment or house is just like a hotel, elegantly furnished and fully furnished, but there is no landlord or host living at the property. You can afford your guests the option to rent out just one bedroom, or two, or the whole house depending on the number of bedrooms that you have in your unit(s). In SA, the kitchen is fully equipped for self-catering with a fridge, a hob, a microwave, pots, pans, etc. - everything you'd expect to find in your own kitchen. This way, the guests have a 'home from home' experience. Serviced accommodation is generally classified into one of the following three broad categories: aparthotels, serviced apartments, and corporate housing. It's important to understand the differences between them as each one has significant differences concerning the strategy, the target market, and the location.

Aparthotels

This kind of serviced accommodation is most similar to a hotel as it offers the same services that most hotels offer. Examples of these services include a 24-hour reception, room service, housekeeping, laundry services, conference/meeting rooms, etc. With this type of accommodation, instead of having a big apartment with a fully fitted kitchen, you will find the rooms fitted with a kitchenette. The rooms on offer will be a bit smaller than what you would find in a studio apartment, but definitely bigger than a standard hotel room. Note, this isn't the type of accommodation that you'll be offering – it's just to make you aware of your competition.

Serviced Apartment

This is typically an ordinary apartment that has been converted and furnished specifically for serviced accommodation use. There is no dedicated reception as in aparthotels, so smart R2R'ers like us will use a **key drop service**, or a simple **lockbox fitted to the exterior of the apartment** building or house. This will ensure that we don't spend hours each week driving to and from the property to meet up with the guests to hand over the keys. That's not how the clever operators who value their time, do business. Such an apartment is typically more spacious than what you can find at a hotel, with a dedicated kitchen space that is fully equipped, a living room/dining area, and a bedroom, or bedrooms depending on how big the apartment or house is. The intended feel for this type of serviced accommodation is a 'home away from home'. Your guests will have complete privacy and all the comforts that they could possibly want in an apartment or house, including cooking their own meals, doing their laundry, etc. A serviced apartment is a more comfortable and cheaper alternative for guests - compared to hotels – which don't offer reduced nightly rates for more extended stays. As has been alluded too, depending on the location – some serviced accommodation units will be apartments in an apartment block, others will be standalone houses on a typical residential street. This type of serviced accommodation is what this book is all about, and what I'll be teaching you over the following pages.

Corporate Housing

The only difference between this type of serviced accommodation and serviced apartments (above) is the minimum period that a guest can rent the house out for. Corporate housing has a typical minimum stay of one month, though you can get some operators who offer stays at a minimum of 14 days. Companies that regularly send their employees to work abroad would prefer to use the same facilities and companies over and over again. This creates a sense of stability for the employees, particularly so, if the accommodation offers spacious living space similar to, if not better than, their own places back home - while minimizing on pricy hotel bills. They know what to expect too. Amenities at these corporate houses are usually better than what is offered at budget hotels, which creates a loyal clientele for those in the corporate serviced accommodation business. Again, depending on the location, the SA unit could be a swanky apartment or a large house. You'll learn all about 'corporate lets' in the coming chapters.

Houses vs Apartments? Which is Superior?

The decision between operating houses or apartments will have different implications on your responsibilities as the serviced accommodation provider and also on the environment that your guests will be staying in. It's not to say that you have to choose one or the other, though – I've personally run both successfully. You just need to find out which you want to start with.

Operating an apartment in a residential building means that you won't have full control of the environment that you want to create for your guests. They will have to share stairs, entrance halls, bin chutes, and on top of that - you cannot control noise levels by other residents. Have you ever lived in an apartment with very thin walls? Most modern buildings are now required to pass thorough sound tests, but if you've ever stayed in older ones, you might recall some sleepless nights as a result of noisy neighbours! If you are considering apartments for SA (and you should!), then you'll have to assess how well the building is managed and how secure the building is. You'll also need to consider any restrictive covenants that your guests will be required to adhere to, e.g., maybe there's a no pets policy, or one parking space per apartment policy. With an apartment, you are restricted to only being able to renovate the interior, and you generally can't make any changes to the structure or walls of the building, without permission from the freeholder.

On the other hand, apartments can sometimes have access to a diverse range of amenities and luxuries than you could typically offer in a house, ran as SA. For example, a swimming pool, an on-site gym, a laundry service, and 24-hour security. You are also likely to have less to think about, as you won't have to worry about cleaning the gutters, windows, external walls or maintaining a garden. Keep in mind though that apartment blocks usually do require landlords or apartment owners to each pay a monthly or annual service charge, to cover the costs of upkeep. The landlord may pass this on to you, as the R2R'er. Location again is of importance for serviced apartments, because if you are closer to areas of interest/business (usually in the city-centre) to high-value guests, you will be able to charge higher prices.

So, how do houses fare as serviced accommodation? A house generally means a garden. With a garden, it means that your clientele is extended to include families who are on holiday - who have children that want to play in the garden. You will also attract guests who enjoy being in nature and appreciate accommodation that has such possibilities. A house also means more space that you can use to generate income. How often do you see a five-bedroom apartment? It's not so rare to come across a house that has so many bedrooms. I remember when our entire family went to my Nephew's graduation, a few years back, in Sheffield – all 15 of us managed to fit into a house that we rented for a couple of nights on Airbnb! I won't say the price for those two nights, but let's just say the Airbnb host was rolling in cash!

In a house, you certainly get more living space that you can use resourcefully to create both more value for your guests, and more revenue for you. Remember, in business; we earn in proportion to the value we provide. Maintenance costs vary depending on a multitude of factors, so it would be hard to say whether they'll be higher or lower than the service charges for a serviced apartment. As you know, the location of your property will also determine how easily you attract guests. Most houses are located on the outskirts of the city centre, which implies a longer commute for your guests whose main business could be in the CBD (Central Business District). Alternatively, if your guests prefer long hikes or nature parks, then being out of the city might be exactly what some guests are looking for! As I say, I've had success with both – but I tend to lean toward houses being my preferred option.

Four Models of Serviced Accommodation

Guaranteed Rent Model

The most common (and in my opinion, best) model of Rent to Rent Serviced Accommodation is 'Guaranteed Rent'. It's the one that most people in property circles are inadvertently referring to when they talk about Rent to Rent. With this model, the landlord, who is the owner of the property you are interested in, will let you use his or her property as serviced accommodation in return for a fixed, guaranteed monthly payment. The landlord is typically hands-off in the deal and wants nothing to do with the deal, except to get his cheque each month. He/she is not involved in the provision of the serviced accommodation in any way, other than allowing you to use the property. Either you or the Landlord will cover the costs of small improvement works to bring the property up to a suitable standard – it all comes down to your ability to negotiate during the deal-making phase.

In addition, you'll need to ensure that you generate enough bookings each and every month to cover the guaranteed monthly payment to the LL, and the other costs involved in the provision of the serviced accommodation. These costs include marketing the property, paying for utilities, providing for maintenance and repairs as needed, and paying for services such as cleaning, laundry, linen etc. If in any month, you are not able to make enough income to cover all of these costs, the landlord's rent will still be payable, and you will have to cover the shortfall out of your own pocket. The business risk is therefore mostly centred on you, while the landlords only real liability is you, the R2R'er, not paying. The landlord must trust in your ability to make the payment each month. This book will give you all of the knowledge and confidence to make that happen! By the way, **negotiating a month's free rent** with the LL is a great way to get some time to set the deal up, before your financial obligations to the LL begin. Hopefully, your business does exceptionally well, and you are able to make significant profits every month, but remember - the landlord's rent remains fixed. Ever heard of the saying "low risk, low return"? In this case, the landlord is not assuming much risk, and as such, he's taking a pay cut on the rent he could actually get him/herself, by doing the hard work himself. Just for clarification, this is the model that I've always used and the one that I'd recommend to you too!

Landlord JV Model

In this model, you work more closely with the landlord and each share all of the property's expenses, and similarly, all the profits. Think of it this way, the landlord has a property, and you have the business idea. You then take into account all costs involved in maintaining and managing the property. These costs, which under the guaranteed rent model – some were agreed to be covered by the landlord, and others by you – are instead now shared equally. Profits are then split on a 50-50 basis. As can be seen in this structure, the landlord has a direct interest in how the business performs, since he/she can make more money. Risks are also now shared equally. One advantage of this model to you, is that since the landlord puts up the money needed to renovate the house or apartment (in most cases), you are no longer limited by the lack of capital in designing a place which is very attractive. This opens up your clientele as your SA unit is likely to appeal to high-end customers, thus allowing you to charge higher nightly rates.

Alternatively, you can come up with any number of different partnership structures. Maybe you want a 60 /40 or 70 /30 split, or maybe want to be paid a small percentage of the profits, as the managing agent? (see management model)

A key thing to remember with this model is that these deals will usually be harder to find compared to the guaranteed rent model. In the guaranteed rent model, the big attraction for landlords is that he or she wants to forget about the stress that the property has been causing them, and so they want to leave the hassle to somebody else and thereby don't mind surrendering their profit margin. With the profit-split model, the R2R'er doesn't bring all that much to the table which the Landlord couldn't do on their own. For this reason, these JV deals are few and far between, although they can be lucrative for the R2R'er if you're able to find the right deal. Keep reading, and you'll discover exactly how to source deals in the all-important Chapters 3 & 4.

Sourcer JV Model

In this model, there are three people involved in the deal. There is the landlord, who enters into a guaranteed rent agreement with the individual who came up with the serviced accommodation idea and then sold that idea to the landlord. This person is known as the Sourcer. The sourcer then sells the agreement to another investor, who wants to get into the serviced accommodation business - for a one-time-fee, usually £2000-3000. Many people don't have the skills or time to find and land the deals for themselves, so if you can play this part – you can get paid handsomely. While it's not my chosen strategy, some of my 'property friends' are selling 2-4 deals per month and making upwards of £10,000 per month, with minimal risk. Once you develop the skill of sourcing and locking-in deals, you can of course keep them for yourself, or pass them onto others for a tasty fee! Deal sourcing will be covered in much more detail in Chapter 9.

Management Model

This is one of the models in which you have the lowest risk, but often also the lowest reward. You would enter into an agreement with the landlord to manage their property as serviced accommodation, in return for a small percentage of their sales, or turnover. Note, the difference here compared with the other models is that you only get a percentage of revenue, not profits. If, for example, you agree on a rate of 10%, and you secure bookings of £4000 for one month, your earnings would be £400. You will receive this commission irrespective of whether the landlord makes a profit or not. You will be taking on the role of a managing agent, and you are doing the business on behalf of the landlord in return for a flat percentage commission. The best thing about this model is that you can't lose money – even if the property has a bad month of bookings. Of course, it's in both yours and the landlord's best interest to bring in as much money as possible, though. It's a great model, but it's more hands-on, and can quickly become a job, the exact thing that you're running away from by going into business!

Doing Your Research

Supply and Demand for Serviced Accommodation in Your Area

To get started, take *any* area in which you are interested in operating. What you'll want to determine is the following:

- Is there a demand for serviced accommodation?

- How much serviced accommodation is already supplied in that area?

These two factors – supply and demand for serviced accommodation, will play a significant role in determining how successful you are likely to be in any given location. Supply and demand of serviced accommodation determine the nightly rates that you can charge. Let's say demand is high and supply is low (i.e. Central

London), rentals are likely to be high in that area, and occupancy rates are also likely to be high. If supply is high and demand is low, nightly prices are likely to be lower, making it hard to forecast consistent monthly profits. To assess potential demand, there are several factors that you'll need to consider as you do your research:

- Tourist attractions - The ever-glorious internet will come to your rescue in this regard. What you are looking for as you search are local attractions such as museums, castles, amusement or theme parks, botanical gardens, zoos, lakes, world heritage sites, etc.

- Hospitals - Major hospitals cater to unwell patients. Visiting family members may need nearby accommodation while their loved ones are being treated. The average hospital stay in the UK is seven days, according to the NHS Confederation. This shows that there is likely to be a consistent demand for accommodation in areas close to hospitals. This demand is also *not* seasonal, and if you get a place nearby to a major hospital, you may be able to tap into some of this demand and give some worried families a comfortable place to stay.

- Sporting events - Major football stadiums are also big crowd-drawers. As this book is being written (early 2020), the world is experiencing a never-seen-before global pandemic. It's put a temporary end to all sports events, offices, restaurants, bars, and 100% of tourist attractions across the world. This has caused a big problem for SA operators like myself, and in fact - the stress and boredom it's caused, has partly led me to write this book – so that I feel like I'm still productive and that I'm still adding value to the world by sharing everything I've learned in my journey so far. Let's hope that by the time this book is published, things have returned to normal and that the serviced accommodation is more booming than ever with people eager to get out and see the world, get to work or just explore - after being stuck in isolation for what feels like so long! Anyway, back to what I was saying…

• The UK is home to many huge football stadiums that attract tens of thousands of fans each weekend. Avid football fans look forward to travelling for away matches, and their budget typically stretches to cover accommodation as well as match tickets while on the road to see their favourite teams. Not all fans will stay the night, but a portion will! Serviced accommodation units around stadiums get a big boost every time there is a match, with most fans booking in advance to secure the best apartments or shared houses with their friends.

• Construction - Big construction sites also bring tons of workers into town. Such projects require a broad range of professionals - engineers, executives, consultants, and of course, manual labourers. Each of these groups has different accommodation needs, with some who need access to Wi-Fi and other services. Construction projects can run for years at a time, and as long as they are ongoing, there is likely to be a steady demand for serviced accommodation in that area. Often, in this case, you can use Monday-Friday lets to your advantage. Here, the workers will go back to their regular home at the weekend to see their family, but for them, it's often worth working further from home during the week to make more money than they otherwise could, closer to home. Especially when they can split the cost with other construction workers, it's a far more cost-effective solution than staying in separate hotel rooms!

- Businesses - Business parks will continue to attract people in need of short or medium-stay accommodation. Executives and employees travelling for conferences, training seminars, and for sales-pitches are all likely to need accommodation. P.S. - That's assuming that the whole workforce doesn't adapt to Zoom calls during these times of mass change, but who knows what'll happen – so I'm leaving this one in here!

After confirming potential demand, you should then focus your search more closely by looking at each of these aspects, but in a smaller search area. To check supply, see how many listings there are in a specific area or postcode on AirBnb/Booking.com or any other online travel agent. To check demand, go to some of the calendars of competing properties on Airbnb (posing as a guest) to get an understanding of how many nights are still available, and how many nights already booked. So, which area should you operate in? How you get to that answer is likely to be the product of an iterative research process. Start by choosing a location that you want to operate from and then check if there is anything near that area that brings people in. The closer you can get to these areas, generally the better your cash flow and profits each month will be, because your occupancy levels will be higher. Ideally, you don't want your chosen area to be more than an hour away from where you live currently. In the rare case that you need to visit the property yourself (after set-up), the shorter your journey, the better.

Being Realistic & Defining The Breakeven Point

Ever heard the saying "garbage in, garbage out"? If your research isn't up to the mark, and you make a mistake when estimating potential income from a serviced accommodation unit, you could end up in financial trouble. If your estimated revenue is erroneously high - you may get stuck with a property that doesn't have the capacity to generate enough income. So, as part of doing your research on a potential deal, look for realistic figures that you can use to analyse your deals properly. Remember to use the Deal Analyser Excel Spreadsheet that you can find on page 4.

Look at what your competitors in the area are charging on a nightly basis. Note the average nightly prices, using a spreadsheet. Ensure that you check prices for different-sized apartments, houses, different numbers of rooms, and for different numbers of guests. Work out the average. Then make sure to revisit these figures multiple times throughout the year to track how prices fluctuate. For example, summer will always be the high season with more people needing accommodation for holidays, etc. In April, in Liverpool, when the Grand National takes place, hotels and serviced accommodation providers raise their nightly prices considerably due to the increased demand and increasing number of guests needing to stay in the Aintree area of Liverpool.

The 'breakeven point' is defined as the occupancy percentage you need to make just enough revenue to cover all of your expenses. As such, if you have achieved breakeven, you are not making a profit or a loss. We will go into more detail and examples in the numbers section in Chapter 4. Breakeven occupancy is usually somewhere between 30% - 50%. It really depends on your monthly costs. Nine nights of bookings per month represents a 30% occupancy rate (assuming the average 30-day month). Anything lower will be generating a loss, and anything higher would create a profit. You can also use 'AirDNA' to do some easy online research of your chosen area, but don't take it as fact. It utilizes algorithms and formulas to estimate supply and demand so it's critical that you also carry out your own research, as detailed above.

Other Local Issues to Consider

Before you engage in any property deal, check if there are any local rules and regulations that may hinder you from implementing your Rent to Rent business model, as per your plan. Some of these local issues may impact your ability to operate or may expose you to unexpected costs. I'm not trying to be negative here. I'd just rather be transparent and ensure you know the pitfalls too. A handful of local issues that you will need to check for are listed below:

- HMO licensing which limits the number of tenants that you can sublet to before you need to apply for a license. Look into 'Article 4', too. (Applies more to R2R HMO).

- Building insurance terms and conditions must not forbid sub-letting

- Local regulations to be aware of. For example, London has a 90-day rule that prohibits landlords from renting out their properties as short-stay accommodation for more than 90 days out of a calendar year. In Chapter 10, 'Secrets of the game', I'll give you one method to bypass that rule – so stay tuned and keep your highlighter pen at the ready.

- Furthermore, before you commit to any R2R deal, check the local council's website and give the local housing officers a call to see if there are any local factors to be aware of for new serviced accommodation operators.

• Competition – what are others charging in your area, and how good is their product/service? (accommodation) Do you think you would be able to match their offering and then go beyond it? Always strive to be the best to set yourself apart from the competition. Take note that if you are trying to set up this business in a city you have never stayed, competition is a local factor that you will have to take into account, as nightly rates may be much different to what you initially expected. So take time out to do your due diligence here.

The Lure of Serviced Accommodation Compared to Hotels

A serviced accommodation unit has its own kitchen and usually far more space, compared to a hotel room. On average, a serviced apartment has 30% more space than a hotel room. Often serviced accommodation is cheaper than hotel accommodation, especially for long-term stays. Yet, for a lower price, the guests have a whole apartment with even more facilities! That means that in addition to more space, your guests have separate rooms to sleep, eat, and live - a luxury that is not available in hotels. When longer stays are required, such stays are much cheaper compared to a hotel, as guests can get discounts in SA.

Chapter 3:
Securing Your First Deal

Without an actual deal agreed, you can't yet proudly say that you have set up your Rent to Rent business successfully. This is one of the most important chapters so please take the time to read through it all! If you are raring to go and are itching to lock in your first deal, hold on a bit and ensure that you have addressed the following things first. Do you have a LTD company set up? And are you compliant with all the regulations? Of course, you won't be able to answer this last bit if you are not aware of the regulations that will concern you. So, here are your initial tasks.

Set Up Your Limited Company

Maybe you're just starting Rent to Rent as a side-hustle, or maybe you want to scale the business to six-figures and beyond soon.

Regardless, you'll need to form a limited company. You can easily register one using Companies House at a cost of around £13. You will also need to open a separate business bank account to associate to the company. Doing this will enable you to manage your business better, and is the start of good financial management, as you (or an accountant) will have to prepare a full set of accounts every year. Having a limited company will also enable you to separate your personal assets from those of the company, in case of any legal disputes, and will also allow you to manage your tax liabilities better. You should also draft a Heads of Terms too. It's a document which outlines the key terms of a proposed agreement between parties. When you start approaching landlords with such professionalism, you are and are more likely to get more favourable responses.

Register with the Information Commissioner's Office (ICO)

When operating a Rent to Rent business, you will be handling a whole host of personal data (names, addresses, bank details, etc.) of all of your guests and even potential landlords. All businesses which handle personal information are required by law to register with the ICO and pay an annual fee (based on turnover and their number of employees). This money is used to fund data protection work conducted by the ICO. The fee starts as low as £40 per year, but failure to comply can lead to penalties of up to £4,350! So get your company registered immediately and keep your certificate of proof somewhere safe.

Register with a Redress Scheme

All letting agents and managing agents are required by law to register with a redress scheme. Redress schemes provide customers with a platform to officially make complaints, in the case of an unresolved dispute. In the UK, the two approved redress schemes are The Property Ombudsman (TPO) and the Property Redress Scheme (PRS). Failure to register to at least one scheme may result in a £5,000 fine (Government Digital Service, 2015). When you are running a Rent to Rent business, you are technically a letting agent, marketing to short-stay tenants, collecting their booking fees, and then passing on what is due to the landlord. Applying to be a member of one of these schemes is also a way to demonstrate your commitment to professional standards. Membership fees vary depending on the scale of the business you will be operating and the scheme you choose, so take a look at either the PRS or TPO website for more information.

Client Money Protection Scheme

It is also mandatory for all letting or property management agents to join a Client Money Protection Scheme. This is to ensure that landlords and tenants have recourse in case of failure to repay any money owed. Failure to join a CMP scheme may result in a £30,000 fine. Some of the approved schemes are namely: Client Money Protect, Money Shield, PropertyMark, RICS, Safeagent, and UKAL. If you are a member, you are mandated to hold your client's money in a separate bank account and to also display the certificate of membership in your office (even if your office is at home!) and display the logo on your website. Failure to display the certificate can attract a £5000 fine.

Fire Safety

This is another area that you must extensively research if you don't want to be liable for paying fines worth tens of thousands of pounds. Or worse, being liable for another person's harm caused by a fire in the property. There are many cases where Landlords have fallen short of regulation, as shown below...

www.citation.co.uk › News › Health & Safety Industry News ▾
'Death risk' landlord jailed for fire safety breaches | Citation
A landlord has been jailed for letting homes which have been described as a 'death risk'. Discover the Health & Safety breaches that led to this verdict.

www.lettingagenttoday.co.uk › breaking-news › landlord-jailed-for-fi... ▾
Landlord jailed for fire safety breaches... - Letting Agent Today
Jul 8, 2015 · Landlord jailed for fire safety breaches ... Reform (Fire Safety) Order 2005 which applies to all non-domestic premises in England and Wales.

www.assured-ltd.co.uk › Industry News ▾
London Landlord Jailed and Fined for Repeated Fire Safety ...
Jan 22, 2018 - London Landlord jailed and fined for renting an uninhabitable property .... Fire and safety breaches were knowingly made by Mr Sahib when he allowed ... and call us on 0845 402 3045 or email sales@assured-ltd.co.uk now!

www.wirralfire.co.uk › landlord-jailed-for-breaching-fire-safety-regul ... ▾
Landlord jailed for breaching fire safety regulations - Wirral ...
Oct 14, 2014 · Landlord jailed for breaching fire safety regulations ... non-domestic and multi-occupancy premises in England and Wales are already forced to ...

www.6pumpcourt.co.uk › news › corner-cutting-landlord-jailed-for-fi... ▾
Corner cutting landlord jailed for fire safety breaches when ...
Aug 30, 2016 · A Grimsby and Cleethorpes landlord, Keith Newsum, with a portfolio of about 20 ... Corner cutting landlord jailed for fire safety breaches when ... http://m. grimsbytelegraph.co.uk/keith-newsum-s-tenants-could-have-died-after-

Regulations you need to be aware of include, but are not limited to: The Housing Act, The Housing Health & Safety Rating System, Furniture and Furnishings Regulations, The regulatory reform (Fire Safety) Order, the Smoke and Carbon Monoxide Alarm Regulations and Building Regulations. The onus is on you to understand all these regulations and the requirements for each.

Insurance

Take out professional indemnity insurance to protect yourself against financial loss, personal injury, or property damage that may result from an error on your behalf. Consider public liability insurance, too. If you employ staff (not necessary for contracted workers, like cleaners), you'll also need to take out Employers Liability Insurance.

Join the NRLA

Joining the National Residential Landlords Association (NRLA) is also a fantastic step to take. They offer on-going support for Landlords. Think of them as a sort of trade-union, who work in your best interest (in most cases!).

Time for Action!

After ensuring that your business is legally compliant - you are finally ready to get out there and secure your first income-producing property! Landing your first property deal requires a plethora of skills, including strong communication, deal analysis and the ability to negotiate.

Before we go into the requirements of what exactly you should be looking for (and just as importantly, what you're not looking for), let's look at where you'll find these deals. An incredible website to start looking for Landlords to speak to, is Spareroom.co.uk. Through the site, you can message Landlords who are advertising empty properties, who might be interested in your R2R proposal. Be careful not to send the same copy-and-pasted message to each LL though, or the website can temporarily limit your profile if they suspect you aren't following their terms of service. You are directly solving the LL's problem by acting as a tenant, who's paying them each month. There are other alternatives, like Openrent, and even Gumtree. Also, be sure to attend local property networking events regularly – they're fantastic places to find stressed out, fed-up Landlords, looking for a solution to their problems. Let's look at where, and who can help you land that all-important first deal.

As well as going out and finding deals on your own accord, there are a number of other avenues where you can also source deals. These include:

- **Letting agents** – Letting agents are professionals who have likely been operating in the area that you are interested in for a considerable amount of time. They know exactly which properties are on the market right now, and might even give you details of landlords that could lead you to a great property deal that's ideal for a Rent to Rent proposal. Be sure to give them some commission, if their lead brings you a deal! This way, they'll call you up right away when they find you another potential Rent to Rent deal – now THAT is sourcing made easy! However, R2R is still a strange concept to some letting agents, but the *general rule of thumb* is that smaller, independent agents will be much more open to the idea than larger chains, who have far more policy and stricter, limiting regulations in place. Letting/Estate agents also understand, down to a street by street level, where demand is high and where supply is low – so even having a sit down over a cup of tea with them can prove invaluable! Letting agents are the backbone and the main source of many

R2R operators deal pipeline – they're extremely valuable.

• **Deal Sourcers** – You'll discover exactly how to become a Deal Sourcer in Chapter 9. These are generally small business owners themselves, who may be able to find the ideal property for you and negotiate a deal as per your terms - for a fee that is typically in the £2-3K range. You can easily find deal sourcers or deal packagers online by searching forums like 'The Property Hub', or on Facebook where there are many property investing groups, each with thousands of members. There's plenty of deal sourcers, and they usually shout from the rooftops about their services, so they're hard to miss! You can also attend local property networking events to connect with other property investors – building a network of likeminded people will help you leaps and bounds. Not only will you find mentors who are experienced in the business (who can give you great advice), but you may also get leads to great properties and referrals to reputable deal sourcers.

Would I recommend using a deal sourcer for your first deal? There are two sides to this argument. But firstly, this will, of course, depend on whether you have enough money to pay for their service (£2-3K), and whether you are confident that you are dealing with a reputable business-person whom you can trust. So, on the one hand - successfully attaining your first deal and getting your first £750+P/M profit coming in can give you heaps of confidence, as well as big credibility - as you can use this deal to show agents and other landlords that you already have a working business model. Arguably, on the other hand, it is useful to build up the skills of finding your own deals first. In the process, not only will you reduce your upfront costs, but you will learn a lot of invaluable lessons that will make you one of the best operators in the

Rent to Rent Serviced Accommodation business.

- **Apartment Developers** – Are another avenue where you could also find your first property deal is through approaching developers with newly built apartments, or those with apartments still being built in the area you are interested in. By contacting property developers with brand new units (who may be struggling to rent out or sell units at their desired prices), you could offer to rent 2+ units with guaranteed rent, so that they have income coming in to finish their project. One way to find such buildings is to walk around your local area looking for new high-rises or apartments under construction, take down the names of the companies and then get in touch. Instead, you could look for new-build apartments for rent/sale through letting agents/estate agents and try to negotiate a deal through the agent, offering to take multiple units at a time – to remove some burden from the developer. This is often deemed a more advanced strategy and so you may sometimes need a deal or two under your belt to prove that you can take on multiple units at once – or else, some damn good negotiation skills!

It's now time to take a look at **what kind of deals you are looking** for here. To put it simply, the absolute prime candidates are Landlords who are tired of managing but don't want to sell their asset (property). It goes without saying that Landlords who are happy managing their current tenants and who aren't struggling for rental income – aren't going to be interested in receiving less rent than they're getting now – and in those cases, there's no problem that you can solve - so leave them be, and focus on solving problems for tired, fed-up landlords! By approaching tired landlords and solving their problem of either empty properties or troublesome tenants – they can still retain ownership of their precious assets. Of course, the exact criteria you'll be looking for will depend on a number of factors – your location, your R2R model, and your desired guest type.

Once you have a list of potential landlords and their contact details, you will then need to call them to find out if they would be willing to rent out their property to your business, on a guaranteed rent model (or whichever model you desire!). This cold calling will require that you sound confident and have answers to any difficult questions that the landlords may have at the tip of your tongue - this is where good communication skills come into it. If you get a tentative 'yes', or a sense of intrigue, arrange a time and date for a viewing right away!

It is important, though, as you start this process to keep in mind that this process won't be easy, and it'll likely take many rejections before you get what you want. If you're nervous on the phone and don't want to blow it, it could be a good idea to practice your pitch and what to say on the phone by **calling out-of-area Landlords** or Letting agents. Keep reading, and I'll keep providing golden nuggets like that!

What to Look for During the R2R Viewing

There are four main things to consider when searching for a property that will make a good Rent to Rent deal.

1) A well-maintained house
2) A freehold property/one with mortgage conditions allowing sub-letting
3) Landlord specific demands…
4) Insurance

The first thing to check for is whether the house in question is in a lettable condition. You should always keep in mind, as you search for an ideal property, that the key to making a profit (which is essentially why you are in business in the first place!) is to maximise revenue and minimise costs. If the house is not in an almost lettable condition, you will have high refurbishment costs (unless the Landlord agrees to cover the costs) to fix the interior of the house to get it to Serviced Accommodation standard. If these costs are too high, the deal won't stack up. Make a checklist of things to look for. A basic list includes a working boiler, solid floorboards, no signs of leaking pipes or other water damage problems, and an intact roof. If the house has some of these problems – you may still be interested in pursuing the deal because of its other merits i.e., proximity to areas of interest, high demand etc. Find out whether the landlord is willing to fix and front the cost for these issues first before you sign any agreements. Be prepared to walk away from a large number of deals that don't meet your criteria.

The second thing that you will have to probe the landlord for is whether the house is an unencumbered property or whether it is still financed on a mortgage. This is important, as some mortgaged properties have a clause that prohibits Rent to Rent arrangements or sub-letting. Failure to adhere to mortgage terms and conditions may mean the landlord is in breach of his/her contract and the mortgage would become void if the lender finds out about the sub-letting. This may lead to the landlord having to immediately repay the loan, failure of which may result in the house being repossessed. Some landlords may not be aware of such mortgage clauses, and so it's morally correct for you to probe to ensure that the landlord is in a position to commit to a Rent to Rent agreement. If mortgage terms do not allow, then stay away from such deals. Alternatively, try to find properties that are unencumbered - meaning there is no mortgage against the property. Fortunately, more than 30% of properties in the UK are unencumbered.

The third thing you must consider is your potential landlord's requirements. Just as much as you may have your plan worked out to a tee – your prospective landlord will have demands too! For example, if the amount of guaranteed rent that you want to pay to the LL doesn't align with how much money the Landlord wants to receive – then it's highly likely that you'll need to take it on the chin and move on to the next deal. In addition to this, if you are considering R2R with apartments, you must check the apartment block's T&C's. Some apartment buildings have rules against short-term rentals in the lease or sales agreements, which may mean that even when your landlord is willing to let the property to you - conducting your serviced accommodation business in some apartment blocks will simply not be allowed.

Finally, does the insurance that the landlord has on the property recognise that the property is allowed to be rented out commercially? If not, there is likely to be a premium that will be charged, or new insurance cover would need to be arranged. Who is going to cover the extra cost? If after accounting for all of the expenses in the deal, your forecasted monthly profit is too low, or you realise that you will have to maintain close to 100% occupancy each month to cover all your costs, then there is no margin of safety in this deal. You are better off walking away and finding a better deal. In Chapter 4, we'll look at the numbers more closely.

Use Break Clauses To Your Advantage

Most Rent to Rent deals are agreed for between three to five years. After you have agreed on terms with the landlord, you should go to a solicitor to get a proper, watertight contract made - rather than using shoddy contracts shared freely on the internet. This will definitely cost you more initially, but the resulting contract is going to be a much stronger legal document that will protect both sides better legally should anything go wrong. Furthermore, you can use the same template again and again in your future deals.

In the contract, you should place 'break clauses', these are a provision that allows any one of the parties to end the deal early. Usually, a break clause is placed at the 6 or 12-month mark. These clauses are there to protect both sides, in case one of the parties no longer wants to work with the other, for whatever reason. Given that you may have invested money into the property by buying furniture and decorating etc. -if the landlord wanted out, you should at least be given a reasonable period to operate the property and recoup the money that you invested. As such, the norm in most contracts is that the landlord cannot break off or quit the deal before six months, to ensure that you as the Rent to Renter has six months' worth of profit to gain back any initial investment that you put in. You should pay attention to notice requirements should there need to invoke the break clause. Also though, imagine this from the Landlords perspective – let's say you took the property on a R2R basis, but then did a shoddy job at managing it – isn't it only fair that he/she can get out of the deal too? I think so.

Chapter 4:
Knowing The Numbers –
Case Studies & Past Deals
Of Mine

Before we dive into this all-important chapter, remember to download the Deal analysis spreadsheet from Page 4. It'll massively help you to 'stack' and analyse deals with ease. Within minutes, you'll know whether a deal is worth pursuing, or not. As you go through this chapter, keep in mind the 6-month rule. The rule simply ensures that your projected profit within the first six months of running the deal should be greater than the amount you've invested into the deal in furniture, decoration, advertising costs and any other money it costs you to enter the deal. This ensures that even if in the unlikely situation where the LL was to execute the 6-

month break clause, you'll still make a profit – and not lose any money.

The 6 Month Rule:

Estimated Monthly Profit x 6 > Total Money You Invest Into Deal

Keep it in mind throughout your deal analysis.

In this Chapter, I want to give you three case studies of my first ever R2R deals – because they span from extremely successful house deals, to not so successful houses, to winning apartments! The full spectrum is covered, so it would purely be a vanity exercise to lecture on and on about each of the 20+ unique deals that I've secured and managed in my R2R career up to now.

I was extremely happy and excited to secure my **first R2R deal** in my hometown of Liverpool. It was a huge weight lifted off mine and my family's shoulders. It gave me a hell of a lot of confidence to go and get deals #2, #3 and #4. Anyway, less of the sob story. In actual fact, my first R2R deal was a house rather than an apartment. I managed to find the landlord through spareroom.co.uk. He was struggling to rent his unencumbered property out on a 12-month basis – to a long-term tenant. After a few messages discussing his pain points (unable to let the property, had some minor damp issues, didn't have the time or the energy to manage the property anymore), we organised a phone call. I conveyed that if he agreed to my newly formed company guaranteeing his rent, I would be able to solve all of his problems *at once*. He'd have money coming in each and every month. I would agree to carry out some minor decoration and to fix the gutters that were causing the interior damp. Furthermore, by taking over the management of the house (before delegating this to a management company for a 15% cut of the revenue) - he'd no longer need to worry about the property as we (my company) had it all under control. We agreed to a 5-year deal. Now let's talk numbers and more importantly, monthly cash flow.

The fixed, guaranteed rent that I agreed to pay to the landlord was £600. Being near to Anfield Football Stadium, I knew that the property was in a tremendous location and that each time a home football match was played, I'd be able to really leverage my nightly rates for those weekends. The house had 3 bedrooms, and apart from the small damp issue – it ultimately didn't need too many changes other than adding some new sofas, bedside tables, and some designer touches. I also ensured that all the curtains in the bedrooms had full 'black-out' lining to ensure that our guests could get a good night's rest. In total, I spent only around £3,000, much of it from credit cards (NOT recommended!) and family and friends. This money was enough to bring the property up to a boutique standard (for the area) that would ensure a high occupancy, so long as my marketing was also up to scratch. Utility and cleaning bills vary by the average occupancy level. Our target demographic was friend groups of 3-7, looking to come to the city for leisure, football matches or for any reason. Even with only 3 bedrooms, you can add further beds and sofa beds to increase capacity, and therefore generate a higher nightly rate when the whole house is rented to groups.

In the first year of managing this property, we managed to maintain an occupancy level of 87%. That corresponded to roughly 26 out of 30/31 possible nights. With an average nightly rate of £110 – for bookings of the entire house, that resulted in average monthly revenue of £2860.

Let's look at the following table to see the full breakdown of all the costs of managing this spacious house on a rent-to-rent serviced accommodation basis.

Case Study #1	Notes	Monthly	
Rent to LL	N/A	£600	
Cleaning	26 Nights @ £15	£390	
Council Tax		£120	
Property Manager	Takes 15% of Revenue	£430	
OTA Commission	10% on average	£286	*OTA=Online Travel Agent, i.e. Airbnb
Utility Bills		£300	
Total Outgoings		£2000	
Total Income (Avg)		£2860	
Monthly Profit	**(Average Month)**	**~£800**	
Investment (-£3000)	Months to Breakeven…	£3000 / 800 = 3.75 Months	Fits the 6 month Criteria Aim (Tick)

Not a bad deal at all when you consider that the vast majority of work is outsourced to the local property manager - leaving me free to spend time with my family, play my new found hobby, golf and focus on the things that I enjoy - knowing that I have a predictable positive cashflow of £700-£900 landing in my business current account every month - from just one SA unit. Hopefully by now, you can see why this business model can be so lucrative, yet so passive at the same time!

My **second** R2R SA deal that I managed to secure was not quite so lucrative. It's important to know that not every business deal you do will be a worldly success. You have to make mistakes in order to learn and improve. The second deal appeared at first, in financial terms, to be a fantastic deal. The major mistake that I made was not ensuring and validating customer demand. The location was a little out of town, and not too close to any major landmarks, tourist attractions or business districts. This meant that I had to offer our (the company's) property out at a lower average nightly price than we would have otherwise liked. My initial research indicated that I would be able to charge anywhere from £70-£90 per night for this 3-bedroom house. It was the <u>demand</u> that I failed to do my due diligence on. So, to maintain a high occupancy level - we had to drop our prices to around £50-£60 per night. This meant that our average monthly profit in the first year of running this house was roughly £250. I decided to activate the break clause on my side of the contractual agreement after 12 months - it just wasn't worth my time/effort and wasn't worth the risk of having months in the red (negative cash flow)! The Landlord and I are still on good terms, and he's found a long-term tenant instead, so everybody is happy.

The biggest take-away from this project is to your research and due-diligence PROPERLY. What I learned here was to test demand better. There are many ways that I now do this, which you can utilise too. One way to test demand is to run <u>dummy</u> <u>advertisements</u>. You can create a listing on Airbnb (which would require your approval before any guests can actually pay you) - so guests are effectively requesting to stay at your 'dummy property'. On the dummy listing, use a random postcode nearby to a potential deal you are considering, use good quality interior pictures, and ensure the description is up to scratch (more on that later). This will give you a strong indication of how many nights you may be able to fill the property for, each month.

A second tactic you could implement to test a property, or an areas demand is to look at the calendars for availability of competing properties in your target area. You can do this on both Airbnb and Booking.com. When I recently went on holiday to Bali, some of the best performing Villa's had their Airbnb calendars booked up for more than 3 months in advance (in the off-season)! A further option is speaking to delegates attending property networking events in your local town or city – these people can also give you a great indication of how their property businesses are performing, and people at these events are often keen to share their successes and failures. You'll be able to take away nuggets of areas to avoid as well as areas to double down on, for your Serviced Accommodation business.

My **third** R2RSA deal was a great success. Having learned from the successes of my first deal, and the downfalls of the second - I was primed and ready to make this third deal my best yet! This time, my company agreed to take over the management of a Liverpool City-Centre apartment. This was a completely new approach for me, but the principles I'd learned from managing the two houses applied equally well to managing apartments.

The apartment was perfectly situated to attract a lot of high paying guests. Right by the party streets, near to a hospital for tired families needing a place to sleep, close to the business district and again, not a million miles away from the two football stadiums in the city. In property, the saying 'location, location, location' exists for a reason - because it's SUPER IMPORTANT. The landlord agreed to a fixed, guaranteed rental payment each month of £600, for an initial period of 4 years. We still have this apartment under contract to this day. This apartment boasts even higher occupancy figures than the first deal we did. Mind you, it's not filled during this pandemic we are faced with in early 2020 - at the time of writing. Over the quieter winter months, we tend to rent the property to more permanent corporate guests, but of course, nobody is really working at the moment. 'Silverdoor' and similar corporate stay agencies are incredible platforms for securing these long term and high paying clients. When you have customers staying for months at a time, it really helps to increase your average occupancy rates.

Side note: The key reason why Landlords will accept slightly lesser than normal rental

SERVICED ACCOMMODATION SECRETS

payments, is because you, as the R2Rer, are guaranteeing their rent for 3-5 years. There's also no hassle on their end since your company is taking care of all the management. The Landlord simply receives his fixed rent into his bank account every month and doesn't need to spend a minute worrying about his property. For this reason, he or she is happy to take a slight pay cut. Not all landlords are ready to do a R2R deal with you, but there are enough out there for you to build an incredible business off the back of this strategy.

During the entire time that my business has been controlling this deal, we've managed to keep an occupancy level of 92%. That corresponds to roughly 27 or 28 nights out of 30/31 possible nights - which is pretty impressive even if I say so myself. By replicating the strategies and tactics in this book, the same occupancy rates are in reach for you too. With an average nightly rate of £130 (city centre location commands a higher price), that brings our average monthly revenue to £3510.

Case Study #3	Notes	Monthly	
Rent to LL	N/A	£600	
Cleaning	27 Nights @ £15	£405	
Council Tax	Higher Banding In City Centre	£150	
Property Manager	Takes 15% of Revenue	£527	
OTA Commission	10% on average	£351	
Utility Bills		~£375	
Total Outgoings		£2400	
Total Income (Avg)		£3510	

Monthly Profit	(Average Month)	~£1000	
Investment -£4000	Months to Breakeven…	£4000 / 1000 = 4 Months	Fits the 6 month Criteria Aim (Tick)

Hopefully, you've appreciated taking a closer look at the numbers, through some case studies of my past deals. Being able to generate up to £1000 a month from each property under management is nothing short of life-changing. Keep reading, and you'll learn a lot more about choosing clients, setting up the apartment, listing the apartment online, the operational side of things, packaging deals and don't forget – the secrets of the game. There is a whole world of opportunity in the short-stay industry, and I want you to get your slice of the pie.

★★★★★

If you are enjoying reading this book so far, and have learned something from 'Serviced Accommodation Secrets' already, **please consider leaving a glowing review on Amazon.** I always love to see that my readers have benefitted from all the planning, effort and countless evenings that I spent writing this book to share my SA successes and failures with you.

★★★★★

Chapter 5:
Choosing Your Client or
Guest Type

The type of guests you intend to fill your serviced accommodation properties with, will depend on your initial research as to what amenities and attractions are nearby to your chosen area. The main types of guests, or clients, that you'll be targeting in your serviced accommodation business are as follows:

Corporate Long-Stay Guests

These are guests who's stays are typically funded by their companies/employers when they are required to work in another city, maybe to consult for another business, or work on a long and important project. These kinds of guests are awesome because they'll keep your place clean, respect it, and often stay for months at a time.

They're hardly the type of people to throw a party or cause any purposeful damage to the property! Furthermore, these dream clients tend to give you fewer vacancies and therefore, more predictable cash flow for your business.

These guests are, however, on the more demanding end of the spectrum in terms of the kind of service that you will need to deliver to maintain a 5-star rating. You will be catering to people like company executives who have travelled far and wide and have probably stayed in some of the most luxurious hotels. You MUST find a competitive advantage, and ensure your product and service is top-notch. You could consider renting furniture to attain higher-end, modern pieces. By renting it, you can get brand new furniture, often in the latest designs - and when the rental period ends, you just return the furniture and get new items! Your property, in this aspect, will always look fresh, clean, and on point, and will impress even the most finicky guests. You can also do the same with household appliances, e.g., washers, dryers, fridges, dishwashers, etc. This also means that

SERVICED ACCOMMODATION SECRETS

you will usually have access to regular maintenance services on most of these items, thus reducing the number of property management issues that you have to deal with. You could also consider hiring an interior designer for the day, to help you figure out how to decorate your property in such a way that it appeals to high-end guests. These guests are likely to pay a premium if you are prepared to go all out and create high-end, luxurious apartments. One such place to land these dream guests, is through Silverdoor – but bear in mind, Silverdoor often like to see some track record of success, they may want to come and check out the property themselves, and they may also prefer if you have multiple units at the point that you approach them. For this reason, corporate clients aren't the most accessible type of guests for beginners to go after. But once you have some experience and credibility under your belt, these clients pay well and are very little hassle!

Contractors

Contractors are professionals who are brought in to consult or work on a building site. Think architects, electricians, plumbers, bricklayers, and plasterers! Such guests often stay in the apartment or house from Monday to Friday, while on a job/building site far away from where they live. They can be in groups or alone. With each phase of the overall project, different contractors are brought in at different times. Massive construction projects can last for years, and if you play your cards right, you can take advantage of the steady stream of guests needing a place to stay from Monday – Friday. Monday to Friday lets also open up a considerable gap of time over the weekend to get the place clean before they return.

Location is essential, as 99% of these workers would prefer to stay as close as possible to the project site to eliminate the need for travel in a city they are not so familiar with. Equally, they've come all this way to be closer to the job, so they aren't going to want a commute on top of that, every day!

If you have secured a property that is close to a major construction site (or multiple smaller ones), a strategy that works is to visit the site (with your hard hat, of course) and to make the companies aware of your local presence. Make sure that you take plenty of business cards with you that can be easily shared around to different people involved in the project, who may need accommodation immediately or in the future. A brochure which shows clear photos of your property and clearly lists the services and amenities that are available would also be helpful. Ensure that they have your phone number and a method of booking.

Secret strategy time: If you are not keen on this cold-marketing approach, you can also find potential guests by going to hotel car parks in your target area and looking for work vans or builders' vans. Most of these vans will usually have a company logo and contact details, which you will want to note down. With this list, you are well on your way to securing extra contractor guests. You can then start calling or emailing each of these contacts, letting them know the advantages of using serviced accommodation compared to hotels, and maybe send them your website so they can see your high-quality, spacious rooms. They might not have even considered that there was an alternative to small, expensive hotel rooms, without a kitchen!

Leisure/Holiday/Family

This is the most prominent, and most common type of guest. The guiding factor for this group, more often than not, when they are choosing accommodation options - is **value** at the cheapest possible cost. If you think you can provide tasteful accommodation options for couples and families, then, while you are still mulling your strategy, spare a moment to search local accommodation options to see what you are up against. There is likely to be fierce competition as these guests have many accommodation options to choose from. To market to this group, the easiest strategy is to list your property on popular online travel agents (which you should be doing for all guest types, regardless!) that have representation in as many countries as possible. This is because potential guests in this group are typically both local and international tourists. As such, the wider the exposure you get, the better.

Groups of Guests

It is common to host large groups of guests if there is a big event nearby, e.g., famous musicians coming to town for a rare concert or a big football match that is about to take place at your local stadium, etc. While you may think that this is good for business (and 95% of the time, it is!), you need to be wary of young people who rent serviced accommodation *under the pretext* of being travellers, when really, they only want a party venue. You will need to put some systems in place to protect yourself. One such system is as follows. Let's say that your SA apartment/house is in London, and the person who requests to stay is also from London (you can tell that from their provided ID), this is a telltale sign that they may be planning a party. Such bookings normally occur on the weekend. You have two options here that are entirely down to your discretion, and your gut instinct. You can either take the risk and hike up your price. For the guests, this would still likely be cheaper than hotels in this case, as in a hotel, they would need separate rooms. In this scenario, please also make it clear what your policy is regarding parties, and the associated charges should they break your rules, or your television! Alternatively, you can just decline the booking, and wait for a lower-risk group of travellers to come along – you'll probably sleep better that night by choosing the latter.

Business, Leisure and Work Relocation Guests

Business and leisure guests can be business owners working and living out of town for a while. If you are able to get such guests, and your serviced accommodation is comfortable, they are likely to grace you with their presence for two or three weeks. The same applies to

SERVICED ACCOMMODATION SECRETS

people who are moving house or city. Such people are likely to be in need of a short-stay apartment or house while they search for a longer-term rental, for six months or a year.

Which Is the Best Type of Guest?

The question to ask shouldn't be, 'which is the best type of guest?', but rather 'which is the best type of guest <u>for me</u>?'. The answer will depend primarily on your chosen location of operation, but also on your risk-level, stress-level etc. For example, if you are the type of person to worry, then leisure guests who might be having parties might be a bad idea! If you are in the central business district, in an area where there are a lot of offices nearby, it makes sense to go for corporate guests. If you are a down-to-earth person and live near some building sites, maybe you would enjoy going and chatting to the builders and providing them with a great place to stay? Is your operating area in Devon, near the beach? If so, then most of your clients are likely to be people on holiday, and you will make more money if you market your property effectively to such people.

There is no one size fits all answer! But as you can see, your location should largely be the determining factor when you are looking for property deals and considering guest types. Are there shops nearby where your guests can buy essentials that you don't provide, like food and drink? Are you close to public transport areas, e.g., a train station or a bus stop? If your guests are not driving, this is likely to be another determining feature in determining if any people or groups that you target are going to be interested in booking your property.

In choosing which type of guests to target, you should also consider what is best for profits vs ease of management! For example, longer stays may be better as it's guaranteed profit for a known duration of time. Because you know you'll be making a profit and a healthy cash flow, you can offer a discount for some more extended stays, and this will guarantee high occupancy rates. Often, weekend guests can pay more, but they are more of a risk in terms of damaging or not respecting your accommodation. The bottom line is; you need to reflect on your business strategy, philosophy and desired location before you even make the first move in looking for the ideal property, and at which guests you might prefer to host!

Chapter 6:
Initial Set-Up

The key when setting up your properties or 'units' for the first time is to look for furnishings that will create a luxurious feel, and that are comparable in quality (or ideally better) than other accommodation providers in your area. Aim to beat the budget hotels and other Airbnb hosts. At the same time, you need to create a comfortable space that will give your clients the feeling of a 'home away from home'. While it's obvious that all serviced accommodation hosts provide furniture, kitchenware, utilities, linen, Wi-Fi, a TV etc., you should aim to go above and beyond and set up your first apartment like a pro. Keep in mind that positive ratings and reviews from your first customers will lead to more customers, thus creating a strong online reputation for your business and brand. Below, I have created a comprehensive room-by-room list for you, of pretty much everything that you

should need to include on your shopping list.
IKEA awaits!

Your Shopping List

The Bedrooms

- Bed – Of course, a high-quality mattress will make a big difference in how well your guests sleep at night. Budget beds will need to be replaced time and again, and are just not worth buying compared to good-quality beds that can last for years

- Headboard - Even though your guests can sleep without one, a stylish headboard creates a beautiful, finishing touch to the beds, and has a subtle aesthetic effect. Keep in mind that FIRST IMPRESSIONS matter. If your pictures aren't good quality on the online listings and on your website (more on that later), you'll likely lose a lot of potential bookings

- Bedside table – Somewhere for the guests to place their books, contact lenses etc.

- Bedside lamp – So guests can read or get some low-level light, at any time

- Dresser / Shelves

- Alarm clock – So guests don't miss any important meetings or early-morning events they've paid a lot of money for!

- Dresser with full-length mirror – So guests can look great before meals or events

- Safe – For guests to keep their passports, or money inside of, securely!

- Multiple bins – So that rubbish doesn't end up left on the floor!

- A rug – Creates a homely feel on uninviting hard floors

- Bed linens - Including mattress and pillow protectors - to make sure that your bed and pillows do not get stained, thus extending their lifespan. Good-quality bed linen usually has a minimum of 300-thread count. Your guests will revel in the luxurious feel of good-quality linen. Keep in mind that you will need multiple of the following for each bed - a bottom fitted mattress-protector, sheets, duvet covers and pillowcases

The Lounge

- Workspace - This will require that you have a desk and an office chair to provide for those guests who may want to get some work done

- Couches – Get the most comfortable ones you can afford! Leather is the easiest to clean

- Rugs – Again, for that home away from home, feel

- Coffee table – To display magazines, décor books, or to hold drinks

- Blankets – For extra comfort

- Smart TV – A high-resolution, large flat-screen TV creates an enjoyable viewing experience. Flexibility connectivity creates more ways in which the television can be used - whether to view travel pictures via Wi-Fi or to view their favourite shows if the guest has a Netflix account, for example, or use the television as a second screen for those guests who want to work from the apartment

- Extension Cables – To allow charging of guest's phones/laptops

The Kitchen

- Full-size washer/dryers. Compact washers may save space as they can fit under most countertops, but this always goes with compromising on capacity. If space limitations are not an issue on your property, then consider full-sized washer/dryers as this will allow you to cater to a varied clientele, including guests who may be travelling as a family who would appreciate the convenience of having a full-sized washer/dryer.

- Microwave & Toaster

- Coffee Machine

- All the usual kitchen utensils – Cutlery, Knifes, Pots & Pans etc.

- Tea / Instant Coffee

- Kettle

- Salt / Pepper

- Sugar / Sweetener

- Hand Soap

- Washing Up Liquid

- Bin Bags

- Dustpan & Brush

The Bathroom

- Providing Luxury Soap, Shampoo & Shower gel will be additional extras that guests will be grateful for
- Clean, white bath towels (2 per guest)
- Towel hooks
- Toilet Paper
- Hair Dryer

Consumables to Budget For

Some things simply cannot be re-used, and these will become on-going costs in your business that you will need to budget for on a per-guest basis. Think of these as some of the variable costs of the serviced accommodation business. These costs can be easily forgotten when budgeting, and if you forget to purchase them, they might cost you that extra star rating that you need in your reviews on the OTA's! (Online Travel Agents)

- Tissues
- Toilet Paper
- Shampoo / Shower Gel / Soap / Toothpaste
- Stationery - a simple pen and paper can do, but with time, you can have company-customised stationery. If printed in bulk, the cost will not be huge, and this will add a nice memorable touch. Guests may take these with them, and this will serve as a method of direct advertising to your target market at a very minimal cost, or will also be great reminders for guests to return!
- In the lounge, it would also be good to have stationery items such as colouring books and crayons, playing cards, a chess set and other board games, as well as books and magazines.

The Option to Lease Furniture

The lists of items set out above can be quite expensive. If you realise that your budget falls far short of what you will need, instead of going for substandard furnishings, you can consider renting some of the larger furniture. Many companies offer this service – and usually they'll deliver and build it for you too. Also consider negotiating with the LL to provide upfront capital for some of these items if you have the opportunity to do so.

Going Remote

Make sure that you utilise lockboxes or a key drop service to ensure that you don't become a slave to managing the property and to ensure you don't need to be present to let each of your guests in and out of your SA units. For key drop services, I recommend KeyNest. Alternatively, you can purchase lockboxes in any hardware stores, or online.

Chapter 7:
Setting Up Your Listing, Channel Managers, and Apps

After you have finished setting up your property for serviced accommodation, give it a trial run. Either stay in it yourself, or offer some family or friends a free night in exchange for an honest review and an insight into what you need to improve! Then go ahead and fix anything that you or they discover is amiss. This will ensure that everything is running smoothly before your property goes live. When it's ready to go online, there's what at first seems like an overwhelmingly large number of different sites! In my experience, the best are: Booking.com, Airbnb, hotels.com, lastminute.com, Expedia, and Trivago – and yes, in that order! It's not to say that there's a whole lot wrong with the ones towards the end, but they generally won't bring you as many bookings. Consequently, in this book, we'll primarily be covering Booking.com and Airbnb as these two are the most popular OTA's, and bring in the most revenue. Booking.com covers 228 countries worldwide, so imagine the exposure that your property will get just by listing on there alone!

Should You List on Booking.com or Airbnb?

The answer is straightforward, BOTH! But let's look at the differences between the two services anyway. Booking.com is simply a booking service, where potential guests get to look at available properties and choose the one that they like, and book. There is no interaction with the host, but guests can review the hosts' previous reviews as part of their decision-making process.

Airbnb, on the other hand, brands itself as more than just a booking service. It is a community of hosts and guests, where guests can review hosts after a stay, but hosts also review their guests. If a guest is interested in staying at your property, you can choose not to host him/her if after seeing the guest's reviews, you are not comfortable with them. This is particularly because, many listings on Airbnb are home shares (where there's the landlords, or others living in the property already), and you would only want to share your home with somebody you are comfortable with hosting. This option to reject a booking is not available on Booking.com, although as you might expect, you can cancel a booking. Booking.com is mainly for properties where the host is offsite, and the whole apartment is available for rent. However, this is how you should be running your R2R SA business anyway, so list on both sites. It's easy.

How to Set Up and Open a Host Account on Each of the OTAs (Online Travel Agent)

Each OTA has a slightly different host sign-up process, but they are all easy-to-use and beginner-friendly. In order to sign up, you will need to type in your full name, email address, then choose a password, and then select your property type. There are various 'property type' options on the site, as shown above. This variety should serve to make you aware of the many options that potential guests have when they are looking for a place to stay the night, or month! Worldwide, there are 1.9 million listings on Airbnb, with over 200,000 of those in the UK! For this reason, you should strive to make your property listing stand out as much as possible.

When listing your property, you'll also need:

- The listing name of your property. This is the name that will be seen by potential guests when they search for your property online (secret tip coming soon)

- Contact details for this property, i.e. name and contact number for the person running the property

- Location of the property - this requires the full address for the property, so street address, unit number, suite number, floor number, building name, country/region, and postcode

- Layout and pricing - For each room that you have in your property, you will have to specify the following:

    ○ The apartment type, e.g. single, double, twin, triple, quadruple, family, suite, studio, or apartment

    ○ A descriptive room name to identify each particular room you are describing, e.g., budget single room, single room with garden view, deluxe room with balcony, standard room with shared bathroom, etc.

- o Number of bedrooms that come with the apartment

- o Number of living rooms

- o Number of bathrooms

- o Number of apartments of this type that you have available

- Additional facilities offered to guests - examples of these include parking, breakfast, free Wi-Fi, garden, terrace, non-smoking rooms, hot tub, swimming pools, electric vehicle charging stations and more

- Proof of your address, 2 x forms of ID, etc.

- Photos of the property (more on getting the best photos soon!)

- Policies – i.e. how you intend to handle the following: free cancellation periods, protection against accidental bookings, guest arrival and departure times, whether you allow children and pets, and minimum stay periods

- Payment details – For receiving that all-important revenue!

The details and information you'll need to sign up for each different OTA (i.e. Airbnb, Booking.com, Expedia etc.) will be pretty similar, but take your time and make sure that you enter everything accurately.

Making Your Listing Stand Out

One way that I like to differentiate my listings is simply using Listing Titles that will stand out in the search results. So instead of the headline being the obvious 'Spacious 2-bedroom apartment', or 'Large 5 bed house sleeps 10', I like to write something much more attention grabbing. For example, you could write something like 'The best house on the street', 'Message me for a special offer', or really anything which just makes your listing stand out from the competition. Get creative, and you'll come up with a number of catchy and attention-grabbing listing titles.

Things to Be Aware of That May Be Considered as a Breach of Contract by The OTA's

You should take some time to understand the terms and conditions of the online travel agents that you are signing up to. This will help you manage your property better and reduce the chances of you being in breach of contract with the OTA. For example, on Booking.com, the following are considered as a material breach:

- Failure to pay commissions due to the travel agent on or before the due date

- Posting incorrect accommodation information about your property. The onus is thus on you as the accommodation provider to ensure that what you promise guests online is what they do get. One area to be particularly wary of is a failure to adjust room availability which may lead to overbookings.

- Refusing to accept a reservation at the price shown at the time of reservation

- Overcharging guests

- Charging guests before the guest arrives without the express approval of the guests

- Legitimate and severe complaints from guests

- Trying to tamper with guest reviews. Reviews should only come from guests who have stayed at your property and should be an honest review of the experience.

- Unprofessional, inappropriate or unlawful behaviour towards guests.

Essential Phone Apps to Run Serviced Accommodation

As your business grows, and you have multiple serviced accommodation units, keeping track of daily happenings will become time-consuming and challenging. Having a 'channel manager' will be crucial, but we'll cover precisely why that is towards the end of this Chapter. When you are successful with your first deal, you will want to move on to your second, and your third, etc., and you won't want to spend all of your time managing the first property - so leveraging with technology becomes the way to go. Some great apps for managing your business on the run include Airbnb (an obvious one!), Stripe, Dropbox and Pulse. Also consider HelloSign. I use it to quickly sign documents online. You could also hire a property manager to manage multiple units for you at the same time - for a 10-15% cut of the overall revenue. More on that later. Remember, time is your most valuable asset.

Customer Relationship Management Systems/Software

Customer Relationship Management (CRM) apps will help you to track leads and your progress when hunting for Rent to Rent deals. You should always be looking out for new deals in preparation for handing properties you are managing, back to the landlord at the end of the lease period, in case you don't secure renewals with favourable terms. Below are examples of some of the best CRM systems that can help you manage to keep track of deals in your pipeline.

Juniper Square

Juniper Square allows you to keep your database of contacts in one place. This way, you can track the progress of potential deals easily. It also has investor reporting capabilities, giving you the ability to see how your Rent to Rent deals are performing, once secured. It must be said though, that the site is quite '*Americanised*', so you may be better to go with Less Annoying CRM or Pipedrive!

Less Annoying CRM

This is the best web-app CRM for small businesses and is particularly useful for those new to the Rent to Rent SA business, with only one or a few properties. It has many valuable functionalities built-in, to help those starting out in the property business to manage contacts, property leads and more. You can also make notes on deals, properties under your management, use the calendar, to-do lists, and more. The product is simple and affordable, and all new users currently get a free 30-day trial to see if the app meets their needs.

Agent Hub

Although not a CRM system directly, this is a mobile, multiple listing app that allows you to list, share and even sell your R2R deals to other keen investors. Agent Hub was built exclusively for professionals working in the property sector, e.g. letting agents, freelance agents, property investors, investment advisors, mortgage brokers, etc. Similarly, you can also view properties that are listed by others in the same manner. Through this system, you can quickly note properties that may be of interest if you are intending on scaling your business – which I very much hope that you are! As I say, you may also, in your search for suitable Rent to Rent deals, discover properties that may not quite fit your requirements but may suit someone else, so by selling the contract to them, you'll earn yourself a few thousand pounds.

Best Practises for Photos for the Listings

By now, you've probably heard the saying that, 'a picture is worth a thousand words'. In fact, you've probably heard it far too much – so I'll try not to say it again! However, in the serviced accommodation world, the photos that you use to showcase your property are your most persuasive marketing tool, and will literally make or break your business. Without good, professional photos, you'll be wasting all of your hard work up to this point – and your photos won't show off the property's best features. Without great photos, your bookings will suffer. When a potential guest is looking for a place to stay, after determining how much they are willing to spend, the next thing that they'll do is scroll through listings with availability on preferred dates. Given the wide range of options they'll have, potential guests are usually spoiled for choice.

Before you choose a picture, ask yourself, what it is about the property that you want to showcase? What sets your property apart from your immediate competitors? Potential answers to this question may include a stunning view, a balcony, luxurious furnishings, cleanliness, great facilities, e.g. a swimming pool, lots of parking, or a garden. Make sure your photos showcase these features in the best possible way. If not, then retake the photos until you capture the core essence of your property, or better still, if you want to avoid the photography headache altogether…

The best advice I can give you for your property photos is very simply to use a professional. The average cost for a property photography session in the UK ranges from £90 to £200 depending on the number of photos required and on the size of the property. I usually pay around £120 in the North of England. Some may say in response to this, "That's so expensive!" Well, let me say this. The difference between what you'll manage to take on your iPhone, or even on your DSLR for that matter, and what the professionals can achieve – is enormous. The lighting, the angles, the manual settings. You just won't be able to match the quality of the professional. You've got to stop thinking in the mindset of lack, and start thinking in abundance. You can make the price of the photos back with the profits from just two or three nights of bookings! It's such a small figure in the grand scheme of your business. However, if you are absolutely stubborn, or ultra-short on money – then below, I have listed a few guidelines on how to best take photos yourself. You could, I suppose, book the professional photographer later, once you've had some initial bookings and revenue. If you're using a professional, you won't need to direct him/her – they'll know exactly what to do.

1. Clean your camera lens. Make sure there is no dust or lint.

2. Switch on your grid lines, to centre and balance your picture.

3. Set your camera's focus, and take as many pictures as possible from different perspectives.

4. Make sure your images are crisp and clear. Avoid zooming-in.

5. Use natural light as much as possible. That means avoiding taking your pictures after dark, even when you have a good flash. The flash is best used during the day to soften shadows. Sometimes, opening all the curtains and also switching on all the lights can help you to take clearer pictures.

6. Make sure your photos are in landscape format. This will allow you to capture more of the space that you want to show-off.

7. Make sure that you have photos that feature both the interior and exterior of your property, assuming the outside isn't

unattractive. If so, you might want just to include interior photos.

Pricing Strategies for Serviced Accommodation

Before you list your property online, you need to have worked out your nightly rate. Where should you start, given that you do not have any reviews at this point? While you may be itching to get paid in the shortest possible time and recover any initial capital that you invested into the deal (i.e. for repairs, modifications, furnishings, and marketing) - if your pricing strategy is weak and your price is too high, you will have very high vacancy rates, and you won't reach your desired monthly cashflow. If your price is too low, you might have higher occupancy rates, but then you'll barely make any profit to attain a positive return on investment within the desired time frame, and the deal won't meet the '6-month rule'. The following tips will help you to choose the right price.

1. **What are your competitors charging?** - Check out similar-standard accommodation in your area. How much are they charging? Even if you feel that your property offers more value to guests than what your competitors are charging, it might be a good idea to start by matching your competitors' prices. Deal-seeking guests comparing the properties will choose the one that offers a potentially better deal in the form of bigger rooms, more facilities and amenities, etc. If that happens to be your property, then you will have earned yourself your very first guests! With time, once you have a solid performance record, you can then start raising your prices as reviews are then able to help you market yourself as a higher-end property, to support your higher price level.

2. **Use psychological pricing** – Let's say you wanted to charge around £100 per night, based on your research of your competitors. By simply changing this to read £99, or psychologically even better, £97, you'll get more bookings, just from that one small change! Ever noticed that those overly expensive property training courses are priced at £2997, or £997? Yep, they're using your psychology against you! The research is there to show it works, so you should do it too! In fact, this book that you've just bought was probably listed at £X.99, £X.97 or £X.95, depending on whether you purchased the eBook, Paperback or the Audiobook format!

3. **Niche marketing pricing** - Consider your target market. For example, if you are looking at hosting higher-paying guests - e.g. corporate long-stays, you can charge slightly more than what your competitors are charging. You will then highlight the additional benefits that your property

offers in the description, to justify this higher price. To your target clientele, the high price combined with the added value they are likely to get will reinforce that your unit, is indeed better than the rest, and they will hopefully book your property. To make this work, however, you will have to make sure that you then do deliver on what you've promised, as the guests will come in with high expectations given the premium they would have paid. A higher price also indicates higher perceived value. Think Ford vs. Ferrari. Yes, there's a difference in quality, but is it enough to justify a 10-times price hike? Mostly, it's down to perceived brand value.

4. **Penetration pricing strategy** - This is most suitable for those who are just starting. You may set the price below what your competition is charging, initially, to attract people to your property. After this initial lower price, you can then increase your price to match competitors, or even go

slightly higher. Your service should be impeccable, as the premise of this strategy is to get good reviews that will then justify the higher price later! Social proof is remarkably important.

Other Ways to Market Your SA Unit

There are additional ways other than listing with online travel agents, to market and fill your SA units. Utilizing these different methods will ensure that your property gets maximum visibility and is seen by people, who for whatever reason, aren't using the online travel agents. These options include your own website, email marketing, social media marketing, and even leaflet dropping.

Build Your Own Website

My all-time favourite website builder is WordPress. It's free, and the best around. You can utilise pre-designed and pre-optimised themes to make it really simple, drag and drop-like. There are themes pre-built for serviced accommodation hosts, and you should not need to do any additional coding. There are lots of videos on YouTube to show you how to use WordPress. Be sure to use wordpress.org, not wordpress.com, though, as wordpress.org is superior in every way (for reasons I won't go into here) - and it's free. You'll also need to buy your own domain name, which should match your brand name. Domains are easy to buy, and usually only cost £10 per year.

A well-designed website with a smart layout and ease with which visitors can quickly get what they are looking for, can help you secure more bookings without paying commission to online travel agents, which range from 10% to 25%. Your website is your own platform, where you should go all out in showcasing the beauty of your property, and showcase what guests are likely to experience when they choose your service. There is no limitation here on what you can include, and you can even showcase local attractions that are close to your property, via blog posts. If you combine a well-designed website with good Search Engine Optimisation (SEO) and even paid advertisements, you are likely to rank high in searches when people are searching for local places to stay in your chosen location.

Email Marketing

From your website, encourage visitors to sign up with their email addresses, in exchange for exclusive offers or savings. This will help you to build your email list, that you can then use in your email marketing efforts. As long as the emails that you send are informative, showcase the uniqueness of your property, and end with a strong call for action, you will get high open rates and engagement from this marketing strategy. A call to action is simply something that prompts the reader of your email to do something, e.g. 'click to view availability', or 'click to make a reservation' or 'click to explore other services we have to offer'. By doing email marketing, you'll generate more revenue. Plain and simple.

A very relevant example of email marketing can be seen in the 'lead magnet' that I gave you at the start of this book - the 'R2R SA Deal Analyser'. It's a great thing for both of us, because now, assuming that you downloaded the spreadsheet, I can send you emails about any of my future offers or books, and you - get a free deal analysis spreadsheet to stack up your deals professionally! At the same time, though, don't spam your new email list with rubbish emails, or sell on their information. Also, please look into and be compliant with GDPR.

Social Media Marketing

Run some online giveaways where guests and potential guests can share your social media posts in return for winning a free stay at your property. By doing this, you'll be increasing your following and your brand awareness. Get creative and research social media marketing some more, to get more tips and tricks for growing your following. Furthermore, if you yourself have a large following on social media, you can use that to your advantage and market your properties to your followers directly.

Leafleting

Simply - all you need to do is to design a leaflet showcasing your property. Use Canva. It's free & very user friendly. Have them printed in a printing shop. You can then do what is known as drop marketing, where you just drop off a bunch of leaflets in places where your target clients might see them – or hire some young people to put them through letterboxes in your target area! Make sure they clearly display your beautiful properties and contact details to book. Although, to be honest, I don't use this marketing method anymore, as people who are already living in the area, aren't likely to need short-stay accommodation. The return on investment from this marketing method was never great nor profitable.

Pay Attention to Reviews

Other than on the major OTA's (which are extremely important), your property may also be mentioned and reviewed on third-party sites such as blogs, Trip Advisor, Google local guides, etc. These reviews are often candid and honest comments about your guests' experiences at your property. If you read these, you will get a good idea about what needs to be fixed, what guests like and appreciate, and which further services you could offer to make your guests have the ultimate home-from-home experience. Keep in mind that other fellow guests are more likely to believe these reviews over what you have to say. So, rather than brushing off these comments, acknowledge them and use them to improve. As part of marketing your property, whenever you get a review, whether positive or negative:

- Respond to the reviews. This should be done swiftly (not four weeks later!), and you should take the opportunity to display professionalism in the way you respond.

The way you respond will also demonstrate how well you pay attention to your guests' needs.

- Share the best reviews as part of your marketing materials on your website, social media, email campaigns, etc.

- Should you happen to win an award, include these on your website and in your other promotional materials.

Do You Need a Channel Manager?

Well, the answer to this question really depends on whether you have gone ahead and listed your property on more than one OTA (Online Travel Agent) – which I recommend that you should have! The more avenues where your guests can make bookings, the higher your occupancy rates will be. However, on the flip side, you are also extremely likely to have problems like overbooking and double booking. Two different people viewing your property on different channels may both choose to reserve your property for the same day, and resolving this issue will be problematic - one of the two guests will be left disappointed and awaiting a refund! Assuming that you're listed on both Booking.com & Airbnb for example, and maybe your website too - then there is a big, big need for a channel manager. What a channel manager does, is it enables automatic, simultaneous, real-time updates to room availability, calendar availability, and price. In other words, if on Booking.com, a guest makes a reservation, this will be immediately reflected on your website, and all other channels your property(s) is listed on. That room or property will then be shown as no longer available. The channel manager acts as a central hub where you can change pricing, see your occupancy rates, and much more.

The first big advantage of a channel manager is that everything is synchronised and automated, making it easier to run your property without spending much time on management and manually updating booking platforms. Arguably, you could go ahead and remove availability on each calendar, as and when bookings come in – but it's just not worth the hassle, or time. Even if you sit by your laptop or phone all day – the chances are, you'd still make mistakes. With a channel manager, you will have the freedom to market your property on different platforms, without being overwhelmed. It's also far easier to manage multiple properties, and therefore to scale your business.

Examples of channel managers include Tokeet, Guesty, Kigo, Eviivo, etc. My personal favourite, and the one that I've been with since the start, is Tokeet. The channel manager that you choose to use will depend, of course, on your budget, it's usability, the number of properties that you have under contract, and an array of other factors. Keep in mind that you don't need to set up your channel manager UNTIL you have set up all of your listings on each of your chosen OTA's and your website. Because remember, the point of the channel manager is to bring all of the data and different calendars into one place. Whichever channel manager you choose, their site will show you how to get started through their help pages, support team, or videos.

Chapter 8:
Operations

'Operations' simply refers to the day-to-day running of your serviced accommodation units, in a bid to create an environment that's conducive to giving a pleasant guest experience. Operations covers all aspects of providing services, i.e. preparing for the arrival of guests, ensuring the guests have everything they need, maintaining communication, and then cleaning up after they have checked out – ready for the next guest! It's a repeatable cycle that can be easily systemised and therefore automated, to leverage and free up your time.

Three main options are available to you here. The first option is to take on all, or the majority of the operations yourself. You can be there, at the property(s) overseeing any contractors that you may or may not have hired, e.g. cleaners etc. You would also personally meet and greet all of the guests, and be on hand to respond to any issues or requests that they may have. You'd need to strip the bedding, wash it at home, and then get the rooms ready for the next guests. This ultimately (and unfortunately) means that you would be fully hands-on when it comes to the day to day running of the business, and will have to be available to make decisions on how to manage things, 24 hours a day. Not the best option if you want to scale your R2R SA business, since you're effectively back to trading your time for money, like a 9-5 job. But maybe if you're retired, and wouldn't mind being there for your guests, giving you something to do – then this is an option.

The second option you have is to hire a management company. Nowadays, this is how I run all of my serviced accommodation units. It took a while to find the right, reputable management company, but I'm glad that I did looking back. This option might seem like it's at the other extreme end of the scale, as it means that you're 95% removed from the day-to-day running of the business. If there is anything that needs attention, the company will step in and handle it on your behalf. This will, of course, be for a fee – a cut of the overall revenue – usually 10-20%. The management company will cover the majority of operations for you, freeing up your time, allowing you to pursue new deals, travel the world, or devote more time to your family and hobbies! The only consideration you need to make is whether your current deals or deals that you are analysing - are strong enough financially that you can afford to take the revenue hit. But hold up...

The third option, and arguably the best option for beginners in SA, is to create a system that makes it easy for you to run the property, remotely. With this option, you are still directly involved with all of the operations, but you will have automated as many things as possible to reduce the need for you to be at the property itself, while still providing your guests with the best experience possible. For this option, think iPhone and web-apps like Zapier, Stripe, Pulse etc. Think cleaners, virtual assistants, and plenty of outsourcing/delegating. With this option you'll avoid paying property management fees, but it won't be quite as easy to get everything systemised and automated. However, in my opinion, it's important to learn things the hard way first – so that you understand the ins and outs of the operations. For your first property deal, I would recommend that you carry out at least some aspects of the management, yourself. When you know exactly how everything works, down to the finest details, you won't get 'wool pulled over your eyes' by a management company. You'll know when they're going wrong or slacking when you do eventually bring in a management company for deals two, three and four. This chapter will therefore discuss operations with option three in mind, as this is what I think that beginners should start with, before later hiring a management company to truly free up your time.

Cleaning

In this section, we'll cover why cleaning is so important and I'll also provide you with a cleaning checklist, but you can probably pass these instructions on to your cleaner because there's no way you should be cleaning the apartment or house yourself. Remember, leverage is the key. Time is the single most important asset you will ever have. Cleaning is one area that you cannot afford to compromise on. You should aim to provide a clean and hygienic environment for your guests. If for any reason, you were to get a below-average cleaning score across multiple reviews - some potential guests who read the listing will bail, crippling your occupancy percentage.

The key to providing a clean environment is not just in the cleaning itself. You should also have 'ease of cleanliness' in mind when looking for a property deal, and also furnishing it. Regardless of which operational management option you choose, if your property and the materials inside it are easy to clean - it's going to take less cleaning effort to get it looking good. Let me give you some examples.

Given a choice between fitted carpets and hard flooring, like laminate - what should you go for? Carpets will provide a warm, cosy ambience, especially in cold areas. They'll make the room look and feel comfortable. You can also choose between various colours and styles to create a luxurious-looking room. On the flip side, carpet is notoriously difficult to clean and costly to replace. It only takes a single glass of red wine dropped on a beautiful cream carpet, before the whole thing will need replacing. Believe me; I've done this at home. Not good. Furthermore, if cleaning is not done thoroughly (even without the wine), carpets can trap dirt, dust and other allergens that could make guests with an allergy or respiratory problem uncomfortable. Hard flooring on the other hand is far easier to maintain and is the better option for serviced accommodation units – so long as it fits in nicely with the other décor and furniture. Small rugs which can be quickly thrown into the washer as part of the cleaning routine, can be placed on hard floors to provide a very clean yet pleasant environment that your guests will appreciate.

You should also use high-quality paint for interior walls where you can. With the right paint, walls can be easily scrubbed as part of the cleaning routine in the event of any dirty marks or stains. Tiling in the kitchen and bathroom tend to make those rooms easier to clean, too.

When it comes to choosing a cleaner, you can't go wrong with a proven, local cleaner. Ask for recommendations on social media and at networking events. However, over the years, the trick that I've learned with cleaners is that you should be very strict and refuse to accept a shoddy service right from the first day. If your cleaners are not doing what they agree to do, and are slacking, change cleaner immediately! Cleanliness is so important in your apartments and houses. You don't want to attract negative reviews over something that can be gotten right so easily.

The type of guests that are staying at the property and how long they're staying for will determine how often you require the cleaners to visit the property. For example, if you're catering to corporate stay clients who are staying for two months – then agreeing to have cleaning take place once or twice a week might suffice. If instead, you're catering to leisure guests in which the groups change each night – you'd need the cleaner to go in and clean daily. You'll need a very flexible cleaning team who will be able to come prepared for the next guests at short notice. To make sure that your next guests always arrive at a very clean house, you can give your cleaner a checklist to tick off, to make sure they have covered all bases. Cleaning is more than just hoovering and mopping up, so this basic checklist below should give you comfort that the cleaner is doing everything as they are supposed to. You can modify it to suit your SA unit's requirements.

Cleaners' Checklist

❏ Strip and vacuum all bedding and pillows. Wash the dirty linen. Replace with clean linen, making sure to include mattresses and pillow protectors.

❏ Empty and wipe down all bins - both the inside and the outside of each bin. Reline bins with clean binbags.

❏ Check if the oven facilities have been used. If used, then make sure that all grime and residue is completely removed and that all trays and utensils are scrubbed and washed.

❏ Give the kitchen a thorough cleaning. Empty all kitchen cupboards and the fridge - wipe them down, restocking supplies if necessary. Wash all pots, pans, cutlery, and utensils. If anything is missing, then replace it from the restocking cupboard. Wash all dishcloths and tea-towels and replace with a clean set. Check if there is enough detergent for guests to use.

❏ Scrub all bathrooms, making sure you also clean the tiles.

❏ Check each tap for leaks. Check also if all sinks have stoppers. If you note any of these things,

SERVICED ACCOMMODATION SECRETS

report them so that they can be attended to right away.

❏ Restock toilet paper and other complimentary toiletries. (Make a list of everything that the cleaner needs to check for specific to your SA house or apartments)

❏ Dust and wipe down all surfaces including tables, counters, clocks, shelves, picture frames, fans, etc.

❏ Check if all appliances are working as they are supposed to, including light bulbs and remote controls.

❏ Check if the in-house manual and Wi-Fi connection instructions are where guests can see them. If you can't find them, replace them from the supply cupboard.

❏ Lastly, clean the floors diligently. Sweep, vacuum, and mop. As you do this, move furniture, including the beds - to clean every inch of the floor.

If you also have a garden, you will have to come up with a detailed list of instructions to ensure that your gardener attends to everything properly.

Reminders

To make sure that everything works like clockwork, you will need to send out reminders, not only one or two but lots of them - to cleaners, laundry suppliers, guests and anybody else that is involved in your operations. Some of these will be done automatically by Airbnb or Booking.com, but others, you will have to develop ways to automate or send manually.

To give you an example of how involving trying to send messages manually is, consider the multiple communication points at which you'll be required to get messages across to your guests. You'll need to communicate with guests before the booking, when they make enquiries and when they make requests to book. Once a booking has been made, you will need to communicate with the guest to confirm the booking, then again with check-in instructions (like codes on doors, where to find keys), and finally to give your guest an in-house manual that can go read before they check-in. When your guest has checked in, you will need to communicate with them again to see if everything is in order and see if they have any additional requests. Just before they check out, you will need to send a message with check-out instructions, ideally the night before. After the guest has checked out, you will also need to send out a message thanking your guest for staying at your property, as well as requesting online reviews and feedback.

If you have more than 5 pre-booking enquiries per day and a lot of short-stay customers, can you imagine just how much time you would spend on these messaging platforms?

Remember that cleaners' jobs also have to be intertwined with guest activity. So, with each booking that's made, the cleaner has to be made aware of check-in/check-out times - so that the house or apartment can be cleaned at the right time. The cleaner can also cater to any specific or unique guest requirements.

Reviews

Reviews are a very important marketing aspect that will ensure you maintain a steady stream of future guests. Even though you need your guests to review you, not all guests will make the effort to do so. So, try to make it easy for your guests to review their stays. Here are my top tips:

> • The most obvious thing to do is to provide an outstanding service that your guests feel that they just have to share with others. If your guests are highly impressed with your property and they feel that went out of your way to make them comfortable, it is most likely that they will want to share their enjoyable experience with others via a review.

- Simply, ask - As part of your automated thank-you message after your guest has checked out, ask them to give you a review on the platform they booked with. Highlight that you would appreciate any feedback about their stay and how you could make the guest experience better. Include links to where they can write their guest reviews so that just by clicking on the link, they are taken to the review page. As part of the checkout, you can also give merchandise, like branded pens, postcards, or other items - these will serve as a reminder of the wonderful stay they had at your property and may prompt them to give you a positive review. Again, depending on the platform that the guest used to book, some platforms will automatically send emails to the customer after they check-out reminding them to review their stay.

- Review your guests - If you are hosting on Airbnb, rate your guests there.

Host reviews show other hosts that the particular guest you are reviewing is not a problematic individual. If you review a guest, they will get an email message informing them about your review, and that might prompt them to review you back.

• Acknowledge possible issues in advance - Even though you may have tried your best to create a wonderful environment for your guests, some things are beyond your control. For example, road works outside or construction work taking place two houses away, etc. There is nothing you can do about some of these aspects, other than describing these issues in your property listing so that your customers know what to expect. Those guests who continue to book, despite these issues, will have done so knowingly and won't be shocked when they get to your property. Instead, they will appreciate your honesty. You should also state if something is missing or broken for full transparency.

● Thank You Notes and Free Stuff - This doesn't have to cost you much money. You could buy a little whiteboard and write a personalised welcome message on it. Your cleaner could do this for you! You can also give your guests something at checkout, e.g. chocolate bars, crackers, or little biscuits, together with a thank you note. Whatever you do here, it will set you apart from numerous other hosts and will impress your guests.

Maintenance

Is there a light bulb that needs to be replaced? A leaky, loud, dripping tap? Appliances that are not working? Most of these things can be easily picked up by your cleaner before your guests arrive. If you make sure that these things are checked periodically, your guests will have very little, if anything at all to report on with regard to maintenance. However, you should always make sure that you have a handyman on standby who can attend to issues on your property promptly should a guest report something. Examples of common maintenance issues that you and your handyman should be prepared to handle are:

• Safety equipment - Are there working batteries in the smoke detectors and CO detectors? If not, they'll bleep, in turn disturbing your guests and causing distress.

• Flooring - Bumps, squeaks, stains and cracks will annoy guests, and if you or your cleaner notice something, have it resolved at the earliest possible opportunity.

• Appliances - Given that serviced accommodation has to be fully furnished, make sure that everything works as it is supposed to. Microwaves, hobs, fridges, washers, dryers, irons, hairdryers. Test everything regularly to make sure it works as it should.

- Plug Sockets - There is nothing that will frustrate a guest more than wanting to charge his/her phone or laptop only to discover that the outlet is not working, or is too far away from beds/couches. Have extension leads available. Also, make sure that you have some spare international adaptors at the property. This will be a welcome addition that many other hosts don't make the effort to provide.

- Light bulbs – Flickering or missing light bulbs and switches that aren't working properly are signs of a poorly maintained property and won't attract favourable reviews.

Managing Guest Activities on Your Property

Assuming that you're not staying on the property with your guests, it's hard to control exactly what they'll get up to once you physically hand over the keys, or once they let themselves in. A clear policy about how guests are expected to behave will go a long way to make guests aware of what they can and can't do. Unfortunately, this on its own does not guarantee that they will conform to the rules. Be prepared for guests who may not take good of your property.

The best way to be prepared for these rare events is to get top-quality insurance that covers malicious damage. Many insurance providers don't provide this, so you will have to be very selective. Failure to insure the property properly will mean either you or the landlord paying out of pocket in the event of any damage. Some hosts also choose to charge security deposits. On the rare occasion that a guest damages your property, this deposit money can then go towards fixing these damages. However, before you do so, check out your local competition and see what the best practice in your area is regarding deposit-taking. Some listing platforms have built-in systems that allow you to reclaim money in the case of purposeful damage.

If you have friendly neighbours next-door to your serviced accommodation units, you can also use them to your advantage. They are your eyes and ears on the ground. They can keep you up to date with what's happening at the property or let you know if they notice anything out of the ordinary. Some hosts also install modern doorbell cameras to check the correct number of guests are entering, but personally I haven't as I'm not sure it's ethical, or even legal!

Chapter 9:
Deal Sourcing and
Packaging

Earlier in Chapter 3, I touched on exactly how to find the perfect Rent to Rent deal. Sourcing deals is the holy-grail and is the starting point for getting your Rent to Rent business off the ground. Even if you have great ideas and big plans for your R2R career, without successfully securing that first deal you can't implement everything you've learned so far, or implement any of your great ideas.

Having successfully negotiated and secured deals for yourself, and having managed those properties for a while – you may find yourself wanting to try something new or you may desire another income stream. Deal sourcing is a fantastic option because it utilises a skill set that you already have (finding deals) and you can be paid handsomely for it - £2000 to £3000+ per deal that you sell on. Furthermore, the chances are that you'll still be actively looking for deals in your target area to take on for yourself – but if you come across a deal that maybe doesn't quite fit your criteria, or is a bit far out from your chosen area, doesn't it make sense to secure the deal anyway and then pass the deal on to another eager investor, for a chunk of cash?

In this chapter, you'll learn the difference between 'deal sourcing' and 'deal packaging', as well as the ins and outs of ensuring full compliance with current deal sourcing regulations.

Deal Sourcing

In the Rent to Rent model, as you weigh up and analyse deals, you may discover gems that would otherwise make good deals, but are just not quite what you were looking for. This may be because you're looking to target a different client type or maybe you don't have sufficient funding to invest in that deal at that moment in time. Having discovered the deal, should you just walk away from these potentially splendid deals given the time you've already spent on them? No! If you can't make the deal work yourself for one reason or another, you can pass it on to someone else who may be interested. Investors who are too busy managing their current portfolio or busy at work, or those who don't yet have the skills to go and secure a deal are prime buyers of these kinds of deals. So, give them what they want! These individuals will be happy to pay as much as £2000-£3000, and sometimes, even more as a finder's fee for such deals. You're getting paid and their problem is solved – so it's a win-win situation for both parties. Deal sourcing isn't limited to R2R either, though – you could do it for land deals (huge commissions!), below-market-value property, and in many other situations.

Deal Packaging

After having successfully negotiated and secured a deal, you have two options:

● Sell the deal as it is, which is essentially an option to transact and take on the rental property – 'sourcing' the deal

● Form the deal into a 'package', and charge more money for it

Deal packaging refers to the second option, whereby the deal seller puts together a complete package for the deal purchaser. In this case, not only does the purchaser get the deal, but they may also get the refurbishment carried out for them, contracts pre-drafted, links to a good legal team, or a whole host of other add-ons. By packaging the deal and making it more attractive, you can charge more for it. You could even give them access to the same management company that you use, making it a completely hands-off R2R investment for the deal purchaser.

New entrants and investors into the property market would typically prefer a packaged deal as it takes much of the hassle out of the investment. In addition to the benefits of buying a sourced deal, which include time-saving and not having to go through the challenging process of negotiating a deal, they also get the peace-of-mind that they are buying a profitable deal, that will generate them positive cash flow each month. Of course, it's up to you, as the deal sourcer or deal packager, to ensure that the deals you sell are *actually* good deals. The goal here is never to rip people off. Instead, the objective is to provide a top-notch product and service.

Compliance in Deal-Sourcing

Regulatory authorities are increasingly becoming more scrutinising of deal sourcers operations. While deal sourcing may have been less understood before and had only a handful of players, deal-sourcing has grown exponentially in recent years as more people look for ways to earn money from property, without owning it. Insurance companies are also coming up with bespoke products created explicitly for deal-sourcing. It has become imperative for any deal sourcer to put regulatory compliance at the top of their agenda.

There are four key facets to compliance one needs to address. These are insurance, dispute resolution, data protection, and AML supervision. For more information about deal-sourcing compliance – I highly recommend that you read the book: *Property Sourcing Compliance – by Tina Walsh*. It was a great help to me when I first decided to sell some of my deals on to other investors. You can find that book on Amazon too. While you're on Amazon, you could even leave a positive review for this R2R book if you've enjoyed it so far! It would make me happy to see great feedback.

Insurance

Property transactions are typically high-value in nature, involving substantial amounts of money. Legal battles arising out of such transactions are equally substantial. As such, your business needs to be insured, particularly for professional indemnity. If you're a member of a professional body such as the NRLA - which you're encouraged to be anyway - they may require a higher minimum level of professional indemnity cover. For added comfort, you may consider getting public liability insurance. Should you have employees on payroll (full-time), i.e. cleaners or in-house managers, you'll also need employer's liability insurance. It is crucial to find and be insured by an insurer who understands the deal sourcing/packaging business model.

Dispute Resolution

As covered earlier in the book, you need to register with either the PRS or the TPO. These dispute resolution platforms allow clients and guests to make complaints to a formal body, should they have any problems they can't resolve with you - it's unlikely to happen but registration is mandatory. It will also give guests confidence when booking your accommodation. The OFT (Office of Fair Trading) also has guidelines relating to Deal Sourcing, which you should take a read through.

Data Protection

Please take some time to look into the new GDPR as it has a small effect on how you are allowed to market your business. For example, you can only send emails to customers (or potential customers) who have opted-in to receiving your emails. Remember, you must also register with the ICO (Information Commissioners Office), as mentioned earlier.

Anti-Money Laundering Supervision

The HMRC is responsible for enforcing anti-money laundering regulations amongst estate agents in the UK. It is a strict requirement in the UK for estate agents (and therefore property managers) to register for anti-money-laundering supervision. Under anti-money-laundering regulations, deal sourcers are classified as estate agents. Failure to register may result in civil and criminal prosecution. Pay special attention when transacting so that you're not used as a conduit in money laundering. If a suspicious transaction is processed through your company and you do not report it, you could face civil and criminal prosecution accompanied by heavy fines.

In conclusion, it is highly important to become compliant in all of these aspects, and more, before your company begins trading. Most importantly, remember that registration is just the beginning. It simply puts you on the radar of regulatory authorities and monitoring bodies. Going forward, you must make sure that you operate within the provisions of the law and within the various guidelines that these institutions set out. Again, read Tina Walsh's incredible book – *Property Sourcing Compliance: Keeping You on The Right Side Of The Law*. You can find it on Amazon. Doing so will ensure that you get everything on point with regards to compliance as a professional deal sourcer.

Top Tips to Become a Successful Deal Sourcer

The #1 key requirement to becoming a

successful deal sourcer is having strong social connections. You need to know who is looking for deals, what kind of deals they are looking for, and in which areas. You are effectively playing the middleman role. Build personal relationships with investors in your chosen operating area. Maintain a strong social media following too. Through social media, I've sold more than 10 deals alone. Some social media platforms are more likely to generate leads for you than others. Facebook and Linked-in are great, but I wouldn't bother with Twitter or Tik-Tok! Your kids are probably dancing on Tik-Tok so it's perhaps not the right audience!

2 - Limit your sourcing activities to your local area. You may be tempted to source deals in multiple regions or even nationwide. But by doing this, you won't be able to apply the necessary due diligence to differentiate a good deal from a bad one – one that you would otherwise have stayed away from. A bad deal will stay in your CRM software for much longer than a good one and can ruin your reputation if somebody does purchase the deal from you. The better the deals you source, the more deals

you'll sell. Moreover, the further you have to travel simply to evaluate a deal, the more time you'll lose when you find yourself unable to sell it.

#3 - Ideally, you should be able to physically view the property. As you pursue potential property deals, you may be asked for a ballpark guaranteed rental figure when you make initial contact with the landlord over the phone. This is essentially meant to screen the time-wasters from securing viewing slots. So, before you pick up that phone, not only should you sound confident, but you should have done your homework to come across as a serious investor.

#4 – When to take payment? From my experience, it's best to take a refundable deposit of 10% upfront when an investor agrees to buy the deal. Once everything is finalised, then you should invoice the investor or client for the remaining 90%. Taking a non-refundable payment upfront comes across as scammy and will steer many potential investors away from you. On the other hand, if you don't take any deposit – you'll likely come across some time wasters who never really intend to follow through and buy the deals.

Chapter 10:
Secrets of the Game

In this section, I'll detail <u>four secrets</u> of the game. These are tips that will give you a huge business advantage over your competitors. Each of these secrets, I've learned the hard way through trial and error. Now you get in on them for free, as a thank-you for getting this far through the book.

The 90-Day Airbnb London Rule

Let's start this chapter off with a bang. Very few people are getting this knowledge unless they too have read this chapter of my book. If you're operating in London, you might know about the 90-day rule. In short, Greater London Properties can't be let out on Airbnb for more than 90 nights per calendar year, without planning permission. However, that doesn't have to mean that you stop collecting revenue after you've reached the 90-day limit. Once you hit the limit, here's what you do. You need to indicate to Airbnb that your listing is now a 90+ day rental. This way, you'll be fully compliant – and Airbnb won't take down your listing. Of course, you won't attract so many guests – but there are still plenty of things you can do.

You should also now:

- During the low season, aim for longer-term bookings over 90 days

- Acquire more direct (on your own website) and repeat bookings from corporate and commercial clients in the UK and abroad.

- Use a range of online platforms to win bookings over the longer-term, such as Booking.com and Spareroom.co.uk, while still staying under the 90-day short-stay threshold.

These tactics not only ensure compliance with the rules but will also maximise your profits throughout the year.

Dynamic Pricing

Supply and demand is Economics 101. It's so simple, but I'll give you the short version regardless. High demand and low supply, means high prices. Low demand with ample supply, means lower prices for the same product or service. This is a fundamental economic concept that you should understand and implement when managing your property in order to maximise revenue and to keep vacancy rates to a minimum.

So, as a result, setting your prices for your serviced accommodation unit is not a one-time decision where you just set a rate of let's say, £97/night and then tick task this off as completed. The nightly rate that you can charge is a very sensitive value that highly depends on the demand for rooms in your area at any given time. The supply of short-stay accommodation is pretty much out of your control unless you can get a monopoly on your local area, and own every single unit (which is unlikely). So, you will have to spend some time monitoring demand and correspondingly adjusting your nightly rates, in order to get as many guests as possible. If demand is high, the majority of other hotels and serviced accommodation units will be fully booked, and so you can increase your prices and still retain a high occupancy. When demand is low, you will be contending with your competitors for a smaller number of customers. So, you should reduce your rates to a competitive level and offer discounts to attract customers and maintain a high occupancy.

How much time do you think you'll need to dedicate to this practice? How would you know whether demand is going to be high or low tomorrow? Or the day after? This means you'd need to be doing a lot of reading and research on upcoming local events, estimating a nightly rate, and then if it's too high/low, tweaking it until you get the optimum. This sounds utterly time consuming and boring, but fortunately, *there's a better way!*

The answer to this conundrum is to use **automatic-pricing software**. Otherwise known as dynamic pricing software, these smart-tools collect and analyse thousands of data points to forecast changes in demand and then recommends the optimum price for you to get maximum occupancy and automatically updates your calendar every day. Not only does this save you from the stress of doing all that research, but it also unlocks time for you to concentrate on other aspects of the business. Now your properties will be priced fairly, relative to the demand, and at a similar level to your competition. So long as your service is unbeatable, and you have good social proof (i.e. reviews), you are likely to get higher occupancy rates at the highest possible nightly price - therefore maximising your monthly revenue, profit, and cashflow! Examples of dynamic pricing software include Beyond Pricing, MarketMinder, PriceLabs, etc. There are lots of options, but just take a look at each of their websites and see which one you prefer. I use PriceLabs but you should still check out the alternatives.

TOMS / VAT

In this one, I'm not going to go into all the details and complexities because I'm not a professional tax advisor, but what I will do is let you know what's possible and point you towards some further resources. In the UK, as soon as a business generates a revenue of over £85,000 within a 12-month period, the business must become VAT Registered, and from then on will need to pay 20% of their total revenue to the HMRC as VAT (Value Added Tax). For those businesses with a small profit margin (i.e. SA operators who have below-average R2R deals, and poor business management) – their business can really take a big hit upon becoming VAT registered. Ideally, the R2R deals that you've negotiated and secured should be strong and your profit margins high. Even still, VAT can seem like a large chunk of revenue to be losing. You'll approach and hit the VAT threshold as soon as you have two or three R2R SA deals with good occupancy. At this point, either your deals will be strong enough that your business can still pay VAT and thrive. And you accept your fiscal obligations. Or, you can still stay within the law – but look for ways to reduce the amount of VAT that's payable.

If that's you, and you're looking to optimize you're the tax aspect of your business – speak to your accountant about TOMS – the Tour Operator Margin Scheme. It can significantly reduce your outgoing VAT payments. As I say, I'm not a professional tax-advisor, so speak to your accountant about how the scheme can help you pay less tax.

Virtual Assistants

The secret here is that hiring employees doesn't have to be expensive. Maybe at some point, you'll feel overwhelmed and think you need some assistance. Is it time to think of renting a physical office and getting local staff in? No! Instead, consider having a remote virtual assistant. Create an extremely detailed manual (in a Word document) of every system you have set up so that it can easily be followed by somebody else and you can be free from 'fire-fighting' in the business, day-to-day. This is what McDonald's has done. They have a system for absolutely everything, from how the tomato ketchup is added to the bun, to how the staff move around the kitchen. Search online for more examples to see just how systemized they are. In effect, a McDonald's burger in Alabama, USA will be identical in looks and taste to a burger in a London McDonald's' restaurant'. This is simply due to the company having such well-documented and implemented systems and manuals. Do you think that the founder of McDonald's could have scaled up to tens of thousands of restaurants without systemisation and outsourcing? Absolutely not.

Instead of taking on everything yourself, you can start delegating tasks like managing your email inbox, shortlisting properties and cold calling Landlords, etc. – to a virtual assistant. Doing this will help you to offload mundane but necessary tasks at a very affordable price leaving you with more free time to attend to strategic planning that will help grow your business. You can hire a VA on onlinejobs.ph (or the many alternatives) for as little as £350 p/m – they will be happy to work 40 hours per week. In the Philippines, on a salary like that – they'll be earning more than nurses and teachers, so in no way would you need to feel guilty about underpaying.

Compare that to the UK, where the minimum wage for a 25+ year old is £8.72.

£8.72 x 40 hours = £348.80 → Roughly £350 for *one week*

A VA from the Philippines → Roughly £350 for *one month*

*That's a **4 X cost saving**. And it's a whole lot simpler to hire a foreign VA, even if only for reduced Tax and Insurance responsibilities. Onlinejobs.ph has a lot of resources and makes it easy to find the right VA for your business.*

'Work ON your business, not IN your business.'

Chapter 11:
Scaling Your Business

'Scaling' your business simply means growing your business. Given that each SA property has a size restriction in terms of the number of rooms, the only way to scale your business is to look for more apartment units/houses to rent out. As you go into business, always keep in mind that at the end of your lease, you will be expected to hand the property back to the landlord. In the case where the Landlord doesn't want to renew the deal for another 3-5 year term with you, where will that leave you? For there to be continuity and growth in your R2RSA business, you will want to be continuously watching and looking out for the next investment opportunity.

When you successfully land your first R2R deal, you will be deep in the learning phase of how to set it up, how to deal with guests, and how to market your business. This will get easier over time, as you gain experience. Now you have proven to yourself that the model works for you, go right ahead and replicate it with another property. If you have one unit, it might be generating you £800 / PM profit. If you had 10 units, you would then be generating £8000 / PM in profit! Scaling, in this sense, simply means securing more apartment units/houses to increase your monthly profit and cash flow. There are additional ways to scale your business, too, though. Let's look at them now.

Management Company or 'In-House' Manager?

As the number of properties in your R2R portfolio increases, you will inevitably need to hire more staff. That not only includes cleaners, and maybe overseas VA's but potentially also a property manager. At this stage, you could either hire a management company who'll take a cut of your revenue – usually 10 or 15%. Alternatively, you could hire a full-time employee who will manage each of the properties for you. Both are fantastic options, and both will free up incredible amounts of your time – so that you can work on your business & not in your business.

The only real consideration while choosing between the two, is cost. You simply need to weigh up which is the most cost-effective option, so just do the numbers. Let's say that you were paying 15% of a £10,000 monthly turnover to the management company – that would be £1,500. That's the same as paying an in-house manager a basic salary of £18,000 per year (£1,500 per month). Although with the full-time salaried employee, you have added tax and insurance responsibilities. Furthermore, if your revenue were to dip, you would still be paying the contracted employee £1,500 per month. In comparison, if your revenue were to dip when using the management company, you'd be paying less commission to the management company. Therefore in this scenario, the management company would be the preferred option. Work out how many units you have, weigh up the extra responsibilities, and then you can make an informed decision about which option to proceed with.

Buying SA Units

As you acquire more and more deals on a Rent to Rent basis, you will eventually get to a point where the cash that you are generating every month is enough for you to set some aside and save up for mortgage deposits. Should your business have a good trading history, your cash flow will be high enough to qualify you for a mortgage. At this point, you can begin buying properties (whether houses or apartments) and then renting them out as short-stay accommodation in the same way.

P.S. - Ensure the lender permits this type of business activity. You can look into serviced accommodation mortgage products – they do exist at the time of writing.

Doing this will not only get you onto the property ladder, but it will also ensure that you don't have to worry so much about renewing deals at the end of their rental terms since you are now the Landlord. This gives you a more secure future with less anxiety. In addition, your profit margins will improve. Mortgage payments tend to be less than guaranteed rental payments. For example, if you no longer have guaranteed rental payments that are due to the landlord, your monthly profit could easily jump from £800 to £1300 in a given month. This increase in profit margin means that your business will be more liquid and therefore more flexible to reinvest even more money, in more property! As a property owner, you could also explore other investment strategies, such as Buy-To-Let – where an entire property is rented out on a long-term tenancy. You could also get into the HMO game, where you as the landlord rent rooms out on a long-term basis to either students or professional workers. Property is a wide-reaching beast, and there are so many ways that you can make a fortune. With that said, it's best to focus on one strategy at a time and become a master of it first – before trying your hand at the next 'shiny penny' that comes along.

Chapter 12:
The Alternative - Rent to Rent HMO

Having read this book, if you think that running a serviced accommodation business rentals just sounds like too much hassle (which it probably would be - if you didn't outsource much of the work), you could explore Rent to Rent HMO. The acronym HMO stands for House in Multiple Occupation, more commonly known as a house-share.

A property is classified as a HMO when it's rented out to more than three different individuals who are not from the same household, at the same time. Facilities like the kitchen and bathroom are shared. Tenancies range from 6 to 12 months on a normal AST (Assured shorthold Tenancy) contract. Should you decide to opt for this type of Rent to Rent business, the first thing that you will need to sort out is the licensing aspect. Running an unlicensed HMO can make you and the landlord liable for an unlimited fine. You will also need to adhere to fire and safety practices. In this regard, you will need to install and maintain smoke alarms, comply with council requirements for updated gas certificates annually, and when requested, provide safety certificates for all electrical appliances. Be sure to research your other obligations too.

Why Consider R2R HMO?

The main reason why R2R HMO can be considered a good alternative is due to the more consistent and predictable cash flow. With SA and nightly rentals, there are high and low seasons, and although cashflow can be tremendously high in many months – it can also be erratic – up and down. It is not uncommon for many people who offer serviced accommodation to invoke the 12-month break-clause in their contracts due to a failure to make consistent cash flow (which is often down to agreeing to poor deals in the first place). Fortunately, now that you've read this book – you should be well placed to be successful in the SA business.

Even though your income with a R2R HMO business might not be quite as high as with R2R SA, it will give you a more predictable income. If you're the kind of person who prefers security, stability and safety – it might be worth looking in more depth at the HMO model.

The Future of Rent to Rent Serviced Accommodation

Before we conclude, let's take a moment to reflect on what the future of the R2R SA world has in store. Maybe you're reading this book in 2022, or 2025. Perhaps the world pandemic of 2020 is now nothing but a distant memory, a mere moment in time. Regardless of when you're reading, as this is being written - the global pandemic is ensuing, and the property world has been put on hold – to say the least.

My hope is that, by the time this book is finished, edited, and published, at least some level of normality will have been restored – and that R2R SA will once again be a booming industry and an incredible business opportunity. Once normality is restored and the travel, work, and leisure industries re-open – my hope is that you are primed and ready to get a big slice of that pie. That's been my entire intention with this book.

In the future, I forecast two main changes or disruptions to the SA business. Right now, in 2020, the short-stay accommodation industry is not very heavily regulated in terms of who can get into it, which rules to follow, etc., etc. More regulation is imminent, and in my opinion, it's welcome – it will keep the bad guys out.

Second, individuals and small businesses like you and I appear to have stumbled across a niche opportunity in short-stay letting. However, over the next 10 or 20 years, as institutional investors pour in and 'build-to-rent', this could eventually squeeze out us 'smaller' operators. Due to economies of scale, institutional players can afford to build multi-story apartment blocks at rock bottom prices, and use the entire blocks as serviced accommodation, therefore increasing the supply massively, and reducing demand and average nightly rates.

As a result, if you have any level of interest in this business model, then NOW is the perfect time to jump in before the barriers of entry become too great.

Conclusion

Firstly, huge congratulations are in order for getting right the way to the end of this book. Not many people achieve that, and it's a fantastic first step on the road to serviced accommodation success. Now you are armed with all the information that you need to go out and secure your first positively cash-flowing rental properties, without needing to even own them! Not having vast sums of money to start with is no longer an excuse. You've learned precisely how to analyse deals, seen example deals of my own and discovered how to set up your units, as well as how to list them online across multiple OTA's to secure maximum bookings and revenue. You've discovered the keys of operations, how to become compliant and sell deals on to other investors, how to scale your business like a pro, and finally, the secrets of the game that nobody else was willing tell you.

If you truly want to make this business work, be like Amazon. Be customer-focused. Provide an unbeatable product, with incredible service to accompany it. Market your property with the skills you've learned in this book, and keep improving and learning as you go along. Be passionate about customer (guest) satisfaction, and you'll get every success that you so desire.

Will this mean working hard? Yes. For your first deal, you will undoubtedly have to do a whole lot of 'fire-fighting', fixing problems and improving your systems. As you move to deals #2, #3, #4 & more – you'll understand the business better, you can begin to outsource to VA's, property management companies, or even an in-house manager to free up your time and create the life you always dreamed of. Mojitos in Miami?

The earning potential from this business model is infinite - your only limits are your stubbornness against systemisation and automation, your lack of belief in yourself, and how adaptable to change you are. Testing times will come – like the current virus pandemic - but the best SA operators, like myself, will adapt and overcome. Those who can evolve, will rise and win.

Remember, however, the ultimate goal as you enter into any property business is to eventually own properties, create passive income and to build generational wealth. Master R2R SA first and foremost, and then begin learning about re-investing your profit into cold, hard, tangible assets like residential property and commercial property. Assets that will pay you for life, regardless of if you are working or not. In this way, you can live your life as you choose, free from the trappings of society – the society that so desperately wants your time to keep you in a box, in a cubicle - working towards somebody else's dream.

If you're ready to escape and live the life of your dreams – get out there, start today and make it happen. Rent to Rent is an incredible platform to begin that journey, so with that, I wish you all of the luck in the world.

Don't beat yourself up if things don't take off right away.

Don't quit when the tough times come.

Do your best, nobody can ever ask any more of you than that.

And most of all, enjoy the process – because in the end, you'll realise - the reward, the trophy, and the happiness – it's all found in the journey.

Yours Sincerely, Hugo Bennings

★★★★★

If you've enjoyed reading this book and have learned something from 'Serviced Accommodation Secrets', **please consider leaving a glowing review on Amazon.** I always love to see that my readers have benefitted from all the planning, effort and countless evenings that I spent writing this book to share my SA successes and failures with you.

★★★★★

Glossary

OTA – Online travel agent

LL – Landlord

R2R – Rent to Rent

SA – Serviced Accommodation

HMO - House in Multiple Occupation

References

AgentHub. (n.d.). Property Management Help and FAQ. Retrieved March 10, 2020, from https://agenthubltd.com/faq/

Booking.com. (n.d.). Booking.com terms and conditions. Retrieved March 10, 2020, from https://admin.booking.com/hotelreg/terms-and-conditions.html?language=en;cc1

Government Digital Service. (2015, March 2). Registering with a redress scheme as a property agent. Retrieved March 5, 2020, from https://www.gov.uk/redress-scheme-estate-agencies

NHS confederation. (2017, July 14). NHS statistics, facts and figures. Retrieved March 4, 2020, from https://www.nhsconfed.org/resources/key-statistics-on-the-nhs

Uprety, M. (2020, January 14). 10 Most Common Negative Reviews and How to Prevent Them. Retrieved March 13, 2020, from https://www.lodgify.com/blog/prevent-negative-reviews/

Walmsley, S. (2018, May 22). GDPR: Do I really need to register with the ICO? Retrieved March 5, 2020, from https://news.rla.org.uk/gdpr-do-i-really-need-to-register-with-the-ico/

Printed in Great Britain
by Amazon